misery- precedes
true knowledge

# The sun rises

# in the evening.

## Monism and quietism in Western culture

by DAVID KIRBY

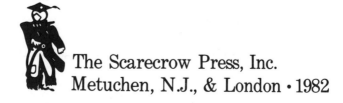

The Scarecrow Press, Inc.
Metuchen, N.J., & London • 1982

Also by David Kirby: America's Hive of Honey, or Foreign
Influences on American Fiction Through Henry James
(Scarecrow, 1980).

PS
374
M543
K57
1982
cop 2

ROBER\_ \_NNING
STROZIE\_ \_3RARY

MAR  -  1991

Tallahassee, Florida

Library of Congress Cataloging in Publication Data

Kirby, David K.
 The sun rises in the evening.

 Includes bibliographical references and index.
 1. American fiction--History and criticism.
2. English fiction--History and criticism.  3. Monism
in literature.  4. Quietism in literature.  5. Monism.
6. Quietism.  I. Title.
PS374.M543K57      823'.009384      82-3247
ISBN 0-8108-1536-2                   AACR2

●

To Barbara

# TABLE OF CONTENTS

Preface

page vii

Ride your horse along the edge of the sword
Hide yourself in the middle of the flames
Blossoms of the fruit tree will bloom in the fire
The sun rises in the evening.

--Zen saying


The realm of art, though dominated by the same
forces as history, always gave more space to
the exceptions--to the heroes of resistance. The
West has always had traditions of quietism in the
arts.

--Martin Green, The Challenge of the Mahatmas

# PREFACE

This book was occasioned by a nagging dissatisfaction with certain literary works, especially (but not entirely) American ones. Why do they end as they do, in uncertainty and darkness? Puzzled readers in our youth, some of us become professors of literature and avoid the question altogether. We urge our own puzzled students to view these troublesome texts with sophistication and tolerance, we point to subtleties of technique and beauties of language, we tell them that the works reflect life, and that life is unfair. But like our students, we want life to be fair. We want it to yield up love, money, peace of mind. We know that our authors have these same human desires, and all our scholarly training aside, some part of us will always wonder why they do not devote more of their imaginative writings to the attainment of them.

It took a wider acquaintance with other disciplines and other cultures before I began to come up with the kinds of answers that I sought. As my view became less parochial, I found to my surprise that I saw my own culture and its literary artifacts more clearly. "Monism" and "quietism" are terms little used by the literary specialist, though they turn up quite frequently in writings on science, history, and philosophy. In a larger sense, monism (the theory) and quietism (the practice) are seen by some as inimical to the Western way of life, predicated as it is on various forms of dualism. In essence, the term "dualism" refers to any philosophical system that explains all phenomena in terms of two distinct principles, such as mind and matter, or good and evil. Typically, dualists are interested in the Other: something they want to attract (money, the opposite sex) or repel (cancer, foreign ideologies). "Monism," in contrast, refers to any philosophical system that views all phenomena as a unified whole. To monists there is no Other--for better or

worse, all is harmony. A simple way to distinguish between
the two outlooks is by means of the verbs emphasized above:
dualists explain actively, monists view quietly.

These are abstract definitions, of course. Paul
Valéry warns us that we cannot get drunk off the labels on
bottles, and these terms will be of the most value to us if
we do not use them statically but instead allow them to help
us understand patterns of behavior that are often complex.
Dualists are active, moralistic, aggressive, involved. Monists are quietistic, contemplative, passive, detached. Yet
neither set of qualities exists in a vacuum. We cannot say
that A is a dualist and B a monist, because each of us manifests both dualistic and monistic tendencies. Further, while
some Westerners will always associate passivity and detachment with hippies, mystics, and Orientals, the fact remains
that both dualistic and monistic qualities are present in all
cultures at all times.

In the West, probably the most important treatment of
monism is the Eden story. One of the strongest urges in
any form of human expression is the desire to return to the
Garden. This desire is found in the Bible, in the Roman
pastoral poets and their latter-day imitators, in Dante and
Milton, in the paintings of Watteau, in the poems of Blake
and Whitman, in the lyrics of the latest pop singer crooning
of a paradise lost that can only be regained by a man and a
woman in naked innocence, inhabitants of a self-sufficient
world, an eternal Now. But an equally strong urge is the
dualistic one--to acquire God's power. This theme, too,
has occasioned much art, from the Bible (again) through
Greek myth, Shakespeare's tragedies, and the Faust story,
as well as such real-life dramas as the rise of Hitler and
the events at Jonestown. That both of these urges have their
locus in the Eden story is an indication that monism and
dualism do indeed coexist, and therefore we deceive ourselves when we listen to, and tell, only half the story.

The first and last chapters of this book are attempts
to suggest the breadth and profundity of my theme. In them,
I discuss monism and quietism primarily in the West, with
emphasis on America, and primarily in religion, philosophy,
and literature, with some attention paid to psychoanalysis,
anthropology, and the popular arts, as well as to the common soil in which these phenomena are rooted, namely, ordinary life. The book concentrates, however, on the interplay in works of literature between monism and dualism.

There are three reasons for this emphasis on literature rather than some other form of expression. In the first place, literature was my point of departure for this study. In the second place, it is both my daily frustration and my daily joy. Even on the days when I am not meeting with students to discuss troublesome works of literature, I am either planning a class or laboring over a review, article, or book about some troublesome work or trying to write a troublesome work of my own (what other kind is worth reading or writing?). Finally, it is through literature that most people encounter the ideas discussed in this book.

I begin with a survey of American cultural history. Insofar as America is what other Western countries want (or at one time wanted) to be, my concentration is there. Too, America is the perfect illustration of my theme; it is quite simply the most obvious triumph of cultural dualism over its perceived, if not actual, opposite. But as indicated by my references in this chapter to other cultures as well as my use in later chapters of literary works from other cultures, the story of that triumph is the story of the West as a whole. To explain why this is the case, and to make my study as broadly applicable as possible, there follows a discussion of developments in the West that underlie the founding of America. From this discussion will emerge a sense of the interrelation of monism and dualism, a sense heightened by an examination of Zen Buddhism, Stoic and Epicurean philosophy, and esoteric Christianity. The chapter concludes with a look at the so-called "philosophers of pessimism" of the nineteenth and early twentieth centuries, here represented by Schopenhauer and, more importantly, Freud--not the mind doctor, but the watchful observer.

Chapter 2 deals with Melville's "Bartleby the Scrivener," the story of a character's principled if bewildering response to the frustrating world of work.

Chapter 3 treats George Eliot's The Mill on the Floss, in which a character undergoes an elaborate if ultimately ineffectual conversion to monistic thought. (As we shall see, there is nothing inherently virtuous about monism, just as there is nothing inherently wrong with the dualism that underlies the bulk of our daily activities--the fault, where there is fault, lies in blindness to monism, not in the failure to embrace it.)

The thought and art of Henry James in general and

The Portrait of a Lady in particular are considered in the next chapter. In a sense, the roots of this essay go back fourteen years, to the time when I was writing a doctoral dissertation on James, marveling at his technical virtuosity as I despaired over what seemed to be so much thematic resignation and passivity. As I have had fourteen years in which to ponder these themes and their full meaning, so different from what I perceived initially, this chapter is the longest one after the introduction.

Chapter 5 discusses Conrad's Heart of Darkness, a master study of Empire gone wrong. In an attempt to explain what happened to both Kurtz and his followers, I make use of the materials now available on the Jonestown tragedy, as well as Francis Ford Coppola's cinematic update of the Conrad story, Apocalypse Now.

Varieties of monism and quietism in the works of several contemporary writers, including Kenneth Rexroth, J. D. Salinger, Joyce Carol Oates, Ralph Ellison, and Mark Strand, are examined in Chapter 6. Had I been restricted throughout this book to an examination of a single author, I believe I would have picked, after Freud and James, who are the greater artists, Rexroth, who is the wider reader and one more thoroughly steeped in both Eastern and Western monism. In his autobiography, Rexroth acknowledges the teachings of the Buddha while asserting that the Stoics and Epicureans are the only wise (as opposed to merely intelligent) philosophers in the West.

Finally, a brief Chapter 7 brings together what has gone before by means of a discussion of two feral children, the Wild Boys of Aveyron and Burundi; their fictional relative Robinson Crusoe; and Crusoe's American cousin, Hank Morgan of A Connecticut Yankee in King Arthur's Court.

The reader may wonder at the absence of certain obvious choices among the authors and works considered. It would have been easy to write on Lawrence and Tolstoy, for example, or a poet like Gary Snyder. But for the most part, I avoid those who have made a career of mysticism and discuss instead authors who grapple with tangible realities. The interrelation of monism and dualism provides a wide range of thematic possibilities, and I have tried to select authors and works that fully demonstrate that range.

★

Parts of this book have appeared in different form in American, British, and Canadian journals. I am grateful to the editors of the following publications for the initial assignments as well as permission to reprint: Change, The Dalhousie Review, The Henry James Review, The Journal of Evolutionary Psychology, Studies in Short Fiction, The Times Literary Supplement, and The Virginia Quarterly Review.

I should like to acknowledge my gratitude to Hunt Hawkins, who guided me toward books and articles on the Novel of Empire in general and Heart of Darkness in particular; Elaine Pagels, who corresponded with me concerning the relation of Christian monism and dualism; and Dennis Todd, whose suggestions helped give the concluding chapter its final form. The students of English 4970, an Honors Seminar on monism and quietism that I taught in the spring of 1981 at Florida State University, asked the kind of questions that led me to be, or at least try to be, clearer than I might have been otherwise. The same is true for an audience to whom I read a portion of this manuscript at the 1982 Conference on Film and Literature, held in Tallahassee and sponsored by the Comparative Literature Circle of Florida State University and the Center for Professional Development and Public Service.

My greatest debt is to Barbara Hamby--my wife, my colleague, my best critic. She spent many long evenings discussing this project with me and going over the manuscript, some of it more than once. It is to her that the book is dedicated.

THE SUN RISES IN THE EVENING
Monism and Quietism in Western Culture

## INTRODUCTION

---

"America is a mistake."

"America is a mistake," said Freud.[1]  We know from his
biography that the condemnation is personal rather than psychoanalytical in nature, for despite the friendly reception
accorded Freud during his visit to this country in 1909 as
well as the recognition given his work, he met inconvenience
and insult everywhere.  Among other things, Freud found
incomprehensible the American propensity for elaborate but
scarce and inaccessible toilet facilities ("they escort you
along miles of corridors and ultimately you are taken to the
very basement, where a marble palace awaits you, only just
in time"[2]).  Sensitive to allusions to his age, Freud was of-
fended when he visited Niagara Falls, only to have the guide
push the other visitors back and say, "Let the old fellow go
first."[3]  He was fifty-three at the time.

But in a larger sense, Freud might have made a legitimate case for saying "America is a mistake" on objective principles.  After all, the basic premise of the science
he founded is that everything is a mistake, or to put it more
accurately, everything is mistaken.  In psychoanalytic terms,
each word, each act, each memory is both itself and something else.  There is a surface reality as well as a deeper
one, and only when we apprehend both realities and the relationship between them can we be said to "take things correctly" rather than mistake them.  Certainly, to be a Jew
in a Christian world is to have a sense of doubleness.  When
Freud was twelve, his father told him of an incident of anti-
Semitic abuse, and at once the young boy thought of Hamil-
car, who made his son Hannibal swear on the household altar
to take revenge on the Romans.  Thereafter, Freud thought
often of Hannibal in his fantasies.[4]  And years later, when
he visited Rome, Freud saw two cities, not one.  As his
biographer tells it:

> There is ancient Rome, in whose culture and history Freud was deeply steeped, the culture that gave birth to European civilization. This alone would appeal powerfully to Freud's interest, which ever turned to the matter of origins and beginnings. Then there is the Christian Rome that destroyed and supplanted the older one. [5]

To Freud, there were two Viennas and two Romes, and to say "America is a mistake" is to suggest that there are two Americas as well. The first is the Republic, the neoclassical façade, the domain of reason; the second is the Romantic dream, the America of the Revolution. [6] Every culture is characterized by a conflict between its public and private wishes, of course, but in America the struggle is particularly stark and visible. There is no other country like America, no other dream as compelling, as dangerous as the American one. America was founded in the spirit of the Enlightenment. In his provocatively titled essay "The Enlightenment and the American Dream," Theodore Hornberger describes this period in intellectual history as

> the sum of the ideas of such men as Bacon, Hobbes, Locke, Newton, Descartes, Montesquieu, Voltaire, and Rousseau. It is the period of the New Science, of deism, of natural rights and natural philosophy, of primitivism and the idea of progress. Its distinguishing mark, perhaps, is a new emphasis upon the good in man, of which the corollary is that man has the power, through his intelligence and his industry, to improve his lot by ever-greater control of his environment.

These are lofty sentiments. Unfortunately, they are inadequate ones, and for two reasons. First, all ideals are subject to contamination once they become widespread, especially in a democracy, where class distinctions cannot operate as a check against those who would manipulate those ideals for their own advantage. The substantive optimism of the thinkers cited by Hornberger becomes the facile optimism of the hucksters lampooned by such American authors as Mark Twain and Sinclair Lewis. Second, a theory of human nature that relies too greatly on the ideas of rationalism and optimism is incomplete. F. O. Matthiessen makes this point in his American Renaissance: "Notwithstanding the humaneness and toleration that make Franklin and Jefferson among the strongest bulwarks in our social heritage," writes Matthiessen, "it is forced inescapably upon us that their rationalism was too shallow to encompass the full complexity of man's nature." Not that Franklin and Jefferson were wrong--they simply were not telling the whole story. Even his biographer notes that Jefferson

> expected citizens to be more reasonable than they are likely to be in any age. He made too little allowance for emotions and counted too much on the sufficiency of reason. In my judgment, as in that of John Adams, he underestimated the evil in unregenerate man, and time has shown that more is needed to cure the ills of mankind than the accumulation of knowledge.

In a sense, the history of American culture has been the attempt to say what Franklin and Jefferson did not or could not say. In Jefferson's words, the purpose of imaginative literature was to present "virtue in the best and vice in the worst forms possible," but such a chillingly rational goal is belied by the works of Hawthorne, Melville, Poe, and the others in the literary pantheon. It is wrong, of course, to say that our major authors are pessimistic, as is often the case. A better word is "anoptimistic," a viewpoint that assumes both the inability to know that all will be well and the impossibility of guaranteeing happy outcomes by the practice of facile optimism.

This fundamental disjunction between the optimists and the anoptimists underlies Richard Chase's observation (in The American Novel and Its Tradition) that "the imagination that produced much of the best and most characteristic American fiction has been shaped by the contradictions and not by the unities and harmonies of our culture." According to Chase, the American novel is different from the English novel because the latter

> has followed a middle way. It is notable for its great practical sanity, its powerful engrossing composition of wide ranges of experience into a moral centrality and equability of judgment.... The profound poetry of disorder we find in the American novel is missing, with rare exceptions, from the English.

Instead, the American novel "has been stirred ... by the aesthetic possibilities of alienation, contradiction, and disorder." Philip Young expands on this idea in Three Bags Full: Essays in American Fiction, where he notes:

> Serious fiction in America has generally operated, at least since Hawthorne, Melville, and Poe, as a reaction against the facile optimisms our country periodically produces. These important writers are all saying, as Melville said that Hawthorne did, "No! in thunder" to the cheerful, affirmative, and often commercial popular views of their times. ... However obvious, it is too often forgotten that our writers live in a society where a kind of idiot optimism is popularly and commercially insisted on. Surrounded as they are by magazine fiction and movies, "family" television, Madison Avenue, and all the rest, they are incessantly driven to try to right the balance--driven by a completely human perversity that reacts in disgust from the piety and cant of an inescapable diet of fake satisfactions and sentimental sorrows. This is an important and often ignored partial accounting for all the misery and sickness you find in our best writers.

Alienation, contradiction, disorder (Chase's terms), misery and sickness (Young's): each of these words is central to the thinking of Sigmund Freud.

★

If America is a mistake, it was certainly not meant to be. No other country has been founded in such a context of premeditation; a work like The Tempest (sometimes called the first work of American literature) is ample evidence of that. The European civilization from which the first explorers and colonizers came had been both formed and informed by the enormous achievements of Christianity, that profoundly goal-oriented religion, on top of which might be added the liberalizing influence of Protestantism, the innovating spirit of the Renaissance, and the exploring vision of modern science. The West was ready for just such a "continent-wide laboratory," to use Daniel Boorstin's phrase, as America proved to be. [7] As a nation, America was a tabula rasa, a blank sheet to be filled in with care. None of the old mistakes would be repeated. None of the rigidity, intolerance, and superstition of the Old World would obtain here. The founders were sure of that, as sure as they were of themselves.

To these founders, the word "self" meant essentially
what it means to us today. When Westerners think of "self,"
they tend to think of a striving, questing entity, one whose
primary purpose is to accomplish things. This self is an
explorer, a scientist. It seeks to discover, to manage, to
compute--witness the embarrassment of those who are baffled
by physics, "don't really understand math," and so on. I
define this scientific self as a Western creature because science is a logical offshoot of a dualistic Greek philosophy that
is Platonic at base, that posits a distinction between subject
and object, the striver and the strived for. As William Barrett observes in The Illusion of Technique, science is a "reckless adventure of the mind."[8] That recklessness is dramatized in the Faust story, a peculiarly Western one. The
Chinese never embarked on that reckless adventure, says
Barrett; no science developed from the fundamentally monistic philosophies of the East. So the concept of self as
scientist/explorer is not only a Western one but also the
only concept that the great majority of Westerners would be
willing to accept.

There is sound historical precedent for this way of
thinking, as evidenced by autobiographical writings in the
West.[9] The first great outpouring of autobiographies came
with the Renaissance and the Reformation. With the decline
of a hierarchical political and economic system in the Middle
Ages, there is increased emphasis on the autonomous individual. In philosophy, Descartes provided an obvious point
of departure with his famous formulation of November 10,
1619: "I think, therefore I am." Narrowly interpreted to
mean "there is no reality other than the mental one," this
dictum was intended by Descartes to express a rather different idea, one perhaps suggested by the less prideful statement "only mind is known directly." But Renaissance Europe
was ready to hear something else. Having long felt inferior
to classical culture and then church culture, it had rediscov-
ered the individual; now Descartes seemed to be saying that
the individual could be--no, must be--the starting point of
any endeavor. The intellectual distance is not great between
Descarte's dictum and Luther's idea of salvation by faith
alone, which frees the individual from both institutional ties
and the performance of good deeds. And as in philosophy
and religion, so in social thought with Rousseau's insistence
on the unique, individual personality, even (perhaps especially) among the "noble savages" thought, in less enlightened
times, to be less than human altogether.

Each of these cultural developments is a way of certi-
fying the importance of self against a rigid and hierarchical
social, economic, and political plan. Each is also an assertion of the self against death. The Black Plague that swept
across Europe in the middle of the fourteenth century, taking
the lives of a third or more of the population, can be seen as
a historical turning point between medieval and modern culture. From India to Iceland, almost every household was
touched. Barbara Tuchman describes the plague symptoms
in detail; the disease began with

> strange black swellings about the size of an egg or
> an apple in the armpits and groin. The swellings
> oozed blood and pus and were followed by spreading
> boils and black blotches on the skin from internal
> bleeding. The sick suffered severe pain and died
> quickly within five days of the first symptoms. As
> the disease spread, other symptoms of continuous
> fever and spitting of blood appeared instead of the
> swellings or buboes. These victims coughed and
> sweated heavily and died even more quickly, within
> three days or less, sometimes in 24 hours. In
> both types everything that issued from the body--
> breath, sweat, blood from the buboes and lungs,
> bloody urine, and blood-blackened excrement--
> smelled foul. Depression and despair accompanied
> the physical symptoms, and before the end "death
> is seen seated on the face."[10]

The peculiar nature of the plague was that it was swift but
not merciful, so that one saw loved ones die horribly yet at
such a rate that often there were not enough living on hand
to bury the dead. Corpses were dragged from homes and
left to putrefy in the streets, sometimes for days at a time.
No wonder that the survivors felt reduced to themselves, un-
aided by spiritual and temporal leaders who were revealed to
be just as mortal as the common run of humanity.

And no wonder that the individual's outlook on life and
death changed radically. In The Divine Comedy, written before the outbreak of plague, Dante journeys through hell, purgatory, and heaven, each of which represents a state of being
after death. But in the sixteenth century, Luther relates hell,
purgatory, and heaven to despair, uncertainty, and assurance.
To Luther, these states have a value that is metaphoric rather
than real; he uses terms that had always been connected with
the afterlife to illuminate life itself. By collapsing Dante's

world in this way, Luther does not gainsay death, but he invites us to become a little more egotistical, to give our lives a little more thought than we might have done in the past.

One can, however, have too much even of a good thing. Looking at autobiographical writing as we move into the eighteenth, nineteenth, and twentieth centuries, we find a loss of confidence in the self. Again, we find writers thinking about death, though by now it seems more like Nietzsche's "pale Criminal," a solitary stalker who waits for the individual rather than a natural force like the plague that cuts down entire populations indiscriminately. Hegel describes death as the "sovereign master," for instance, and Kierkegaard speaks of a "sickness unto death." Individuality becomes isolation, and a sense of loneliness creeps into autobiographical writing; the confident and optimistic sound of "I think, therefore I am" is now discordant and solipsistic. Then, gradually, in the writings of Yeats and Rilke as well as in those of Jung, we perceive a yearning for a wholeness beyond the self, a desire for communion with a God, yes, but a God who is found not in heaven but in the recesses of the psyche.

Yeats, Rilke, and Jung were not inventing something new, however. This yearning for wholeness has been around as long as humanity has. We are less aware of it than we might be because it is an undercurrent that is less noticeable than the events that take place on the tumultuous surface of life. Once we turn away from the demands and frustrations of ordinary living as well as the larger events of history, we are astonished to see how much thought and writing is given over to detachment, to the idea of retreat from externality in order to find peace within. This theme characterizes the personae of Seneca, Epictetus, and Epicurus (whose name has been turned into an adjective synonymous with high living but whose teachings deal more with the avoidance of pain than anything else); the repentant Job and Jonah; Jesus; the Buddha; the Dante of the Paradiso; Augustine; the Fathers of the Egyptian desert; Pascal; the Wordsworth of "Tintern Abbey" and other poems; Keats as self-described in his letters; the couple in Arnold's "Dover Beach"; Emily Dickinson's persona (see "I'm Nobody--Who Are You?" for an example); Alyosha Karamazov; much of Eliot's poetry; Wallace Steven's "The Good Man [Who] Has No Shape"; the protagonist of Borges's story "Everything and Nothing"; the personae of such contemporary poets as W. S. Merwin, Robert Bly, Charles Simic, and Mark Strand, among others; and of course the writings of Yeats, Rilke, and Jung. In America, the country that more

than any other is associated with action and progress, detachment as a literary theme is particularly strong. Among works
of serious literature, the Benjamin Franklin of The Autobiography is the first great mover and shaker but also the last,
for after him come Poe's Pym, the Thoreau of Walden, Hester Prynne, Ishmael, Huckleberry Finn, the Henry Adams of
The Education, the heroes of The Red Badge of Courage and
The Ambassadors and A Farewell to Arms and Catch-22.
All of these are essentially passive or retiring figures in a
world that is too busy for its own good. Students are often
dismayed that the characters in the books they read seem un-
interested in taking charge of their own lives, but the fact
is that most literary heroes and heroines are passive and retiring. Those who are not--Adam, Prometheus, Macbeth,
and Faust are good examples--remind us that action and self-
assertion almost always lead to downfall.

★

In few stories is this interplay between helpful detachment
and harmful self-assertion better illustrated than in the story
of Odysseus, the archetypal hero of Western literature. In
his essay "Odysseus as Hero," Frederic Will observes that
Odysseus rejects the "feminine or effete," that to him "the
feminine principle is dangerous, potentially unreal."[11] To
be feminine, according to Odysseus' way of thinking, is to
be not only effete and unreal but also to be a nothing, a nobody. And to be somebody, to have an identity, is what
Odysseus wants more than anything. In his masterful essay
"The Name of Odysseus," G. E. Dimock, Jr., explains that
Odysseus struggles to be born as he escapes from the cave
of Polyphemus; word-play in the original Greek makes it
clear that not only escape but birth is hinted at in this
scene.[12] In order to escape from the cave of Polyphemus,
Odysseus takes a feminine name: No Man. It is as this
No Man that he escapes.

To put it another way, No Man saves the life of Odysseus, which means that Odysseus would be a fool to disdain
"her." Yet he does, which is to say nothing more than that
Odysseus has much in common with prosaic types like ourselves. Our cult of personality allows us to see only the
glamour of achievement and success; it blinds us to the values of quiet and detachment. Worse, we make all that is
not exclusively masculine into the exclusively effete and contemptible. He who is not a hero is a coward. He who is
not a star is a nobody.

In point of fact, however, if humanity were to be divided into two sets, one of which consisted only of supermasculine Odyssean types, the other would consist not of versions of No Man--a wily, despicable feminized creature who practices her unsavory art on Polyphemus, according to Odysseus, not because it is desirable but because it is necessary--but of versions of Penelope. Odysseus' long-suffering wife is seen by many readers, perhaps the majority, as passive and therefore "typically female." Actually, she is quite active in the sense of ordinary (and a good deal of extraordinary) activity. Year in and year out she handles with consummate grace the importuning of the suitors, keeping them sufficiently ardent but never allowing them to force a choice. She holds things together at home while Odysseus runs around and stirs up trouble in order to create an identity for himself.

Odysseus' problem is that he is essentially a boy. And though it is common to think of him as brave and courageous, we can also view him in the terms that Kenneth Rexroth applies to Odysseus' latter-day imitator, Rimbaud. The story of Rimbaud's life has converted more than one impressionable young person to the life of art, because he seems to be the admirable Brave Adventurer, in both the realm of aesthetics and the real-life realm of adventure in Africa. But Rexroth points out that Rimbaud is not "the very archetype of youth in revolt," even though he appears to be. [13] Rimbaud is not a romantic, but a capitalist, adventurer, an exploiter in the mold of P. T. Barnum and the robber baron Jim Fisk. Rimbaud is a real-life Tom Sawyer, a boy who wants to establish an identity that the bourgeoisie will accept and venerate. Neither Rimbaud nor Tom wants to destroy the bourgeois/capitalist world, as would a true "youth in revolt." They want that world to love them rather than be hostile toward them.

The most convincing proof of Odysseus' childishness is his behavior after he and his companions escape from the cave of Polyphemus. Though they are not yet out of danger, and even though his comrades try to dissuade him, Odysseus decides that he must taunt Polyphemus. Specifically, Odysseus decides that he must reject his feminine aspect, even though it has just saved his life. He must tell Polyphemus that he is not No Man, the wily trickster, but the quintessentially masculine Odysseus, the "sacker of cities." In other words, Odysseus is at last establishing his true identity, but at a great cost. Enraged by Odysseus' taunts, Polyphemus flings boulders at the ship and nearly sinks it. Failing at this, he pronounces the curse that ultimately means death for Odysseus' companions. Polyphemus asks his father, Poseidon, to see to it that, if Odysseus makes it home alive, at least none of his companions survive. And of course that is exactly what happens. Thus, Odysseus becomes Odysseus again and lives up to the promise of his name, which means something like "causer of pain" or perhaps "trouble." Dimock notes that " 'Trouble' is perhaps as good a translation of Odysseus' name as any. When a character in a western movie says, 'Just call me Trouble, stranger,' we take him to be a hostile type who makes trouble for other people."[14]

Yet it could have been otherwise. As he himself demonstrates, Odysseus is both Odysseus and No Man. He chooses the one identity over the other, to the peril of his companions and the grief of his wife. Even that act, however, demonstrates the truth of the psychoanalytic premise with which this chapter began, namely, that everything is itself and something else at the same time. Indeed, both the central idea of this book and its opposite--monism and dualism--are but two aspects of a single premise, two sides of the same philosophical coin. To understand this, we will have to go back to the beginnings of Western philosophy and trace its development.

★

In the West, philosophy begins in the sixth century B. C. with Thales, traditionally the first philosopher and scientist. It is he who is credited with the utterance, "Everything is really water." This paradox expresses the ancient Greek notion that every element contains water, but since the evidence of the five senses contradicts that idea, clearly the statement means much more. According to R. J. Hollingdale, Thales' statement is best explained this way:

> The world we perceive is characterized by great diversity; but this diversity is not fundamental; fundamentally the world is a unity. But notice that this unity is precisely what is not apparent; what is apparent is the reverse, the diversity of the world, and the object of [Thales'] hypothesis is to assert the apparitional nature of this diversity. In its last significance, therefore, "Everything is water" means: (the world of diversity is an apparent world; in reality the world is one.] Thus we find at the very beginning of philosophy

the assertion that there exist two worlds, the "real"
and the "apparent," that everything is "really"
something else and not what it "appears" to be. [15]

What Thales' statement forces us to acknowledge, says Hollingdale, is the "bifurcation of the world into the mundane
world perceived and the transcendent, 'more real' world revealed by thinking." Then why does not Thales say so in the
first place? Because to explain away his own paradox would
be to dilute its difficult yet undeniable implication: that the
world is one and not-one simultaneously.

But as time went by, something interesting happened
to Thales' dictum. Hollingdale writes, "As the [human] race
accumulates experience this world of thinking becomes mas-
sively enriched," especially in contrast to the perceived world.
Now the perceived world is constant. If it seems to change,
that is because the change is cyclical--spring gives way to
summer, but before very long it will be spring again, with
the same quality of light, the same birds, flowers, and so
on. The world of thought, on the other hand, is infinite.
It is thus the only place where people can put the products
of their thinking. So it is only a matter of time before the
world of thought contains gods and devils, heavens and hells.
The world of thought becomes the more important world, the
more real world, and finally the only real world. By Plato's
day, or roughly the fourth century B.C., "the physical universe has been devalued to a shadow-play on the wall....
Everyone knows Plato's parable of the men sitting in a dark
cave with their backs to the light watching the play of their
shadows: the shadows are 'the world,' the light comes from
the 'real world.'"[16]

Platonism is significant to the average Westerner
mainly in that it is the conceptual basis of Christianity. The
bridge between Platonism and Christianity, says Hollingdale,
is the

> so-called Neo-Platonism of Plotinus, in which the
> crumbling Roman Empire is contrasted with the
> supernal realm of beauty and order, which alone is
> asserted to be real. Plotinus's real world is al-
> most the Christian kingdom of this world: all that
> is lacking is a god. With the victory of Christian-
> ity all positive value is transferred to the Beyond.

Thus, Plato drove a wedge between Thales' two worlds

(which, of course, are only one world), and the hammer blows of Christianity made the division complete. "From Paul to Augustine" (that is, from the days of Christ to the fifth century A. D.), notes Hollingdale,

> the history of Christianity is the history of a progressively widening gap between the two worlds, until in its final form Christianity means duality: the duality of Church and State, Pope and Emperor, this world and the next, the City of God and the Earthly City, God and his creation, the individual souls of men and the Holy Spirit "in whom we are all one"--all ultimately forms of that primeval duality of the world in the eyes and the world in the mind."[17]

This duality, first Platonic and then Christian, is so pervasive in our culture that it shapes the thought and speech of even the most unphilosophical and irreligious of us. Whenever the words "thank God" and "go to hell" are uttered, they testify to the number of unwitting disciples of Plotinus and Paul who continue to spread their dualistic gospel.

★

Perhaps it might be said, then, that it is historically correct for Westerners to think and speak dualistically. Certainly it is the most comfortable way for us, as our very language systems tend to be organized in terms of opposites: day/ night, black/white, male/female, good/evil, virtue/vice, our team/their team, and so on. But the intent of this rapid overview of philosophy in the West is to show the inseparable nature, at base, of monism and dualism. (The two outlooks have in common a belief in two worlds, an apparent one and a real one.) (The two outlooks differ in that monists equate the two worlds, the dualists divorce them.) It is as though the monist were saying, "There is an apparent world of diversity and a real world of unity, but since unity runs through diversity (everything is really water), the two worlds are the same." The monist's statement is descriptive rather than judgmental, for one world is not superior to the other. By contrast, the dualist is saying, "This apparent world is an inferior one; somewhere there is a real and superior world where all the important things are." Put simply, both monist and dualist believe in two worlds. To the monist, these worlds are the same; to the dualist, they are different.

Just as it is easy to understand the common basis for the two outlooks, so it is easy to understand the dualist's denial of that commonality. To the list of opposites given above (day/night, etc.) one more pair should be added: dualism/monism. It is the nature of dualism to define the Other, to conquer or at least manage it before it conquers or manages us. Frequently, this tendency is benign. We want to see cancer conquered, for instance, and while we are waiting for the solution to that ill, we can at least be sure that there will never be another outbreak of plague like the one in the Middle Ages, thanks to the preparedness of dedicated dualists in the medical sciences. But the fact remains that this defining and managing tendency, which prompts the dualist to look askance at disease, foreign powers, "the opposite sex," or whatever, also causes the dualist to look with equal suspicion at other philosophies and classify them as alien.

Even when Western intellectuals look favorably on monistic philosophies, they do so in a condescending and sentimental way that only reinforces the false distinction between dualism and monism. Carl Jung is thought to be a great proponent of nonrational, non-Western viewpoints, for instance. Yet even the most cursory examination of his writings reveals that he misunderstands such viewpoints as only a dyed-in-the-wool dualist could. In Memories, Dreams, Reflections, he recalls a midlife meeting with an American Indian who caused the scales to fall from his eyes. This Indian, whom Jung met on a tour of the pueblos in New Mexico, asks the psychoanalyst to contemplate "'how cruel the whites look. Their lips are thin, their noses sharp, their faces furrowed and distorted by folds. Their eyes have a staring expression; they are always seeking something. What are they seeking? The whites always want something; they are always uneasy and restless.'" The problem, continues the Indian, is that the whites "'think with their heads,'" not with their hearts, as the Indians do. On receipt of this news, recalls Jung, "I fell into a long meditation. For the first time in my life, so it seemed to me, someone had drawn for me a picture of the real white man. It was as though until now I had seen nothing but sentimental, prettified color prints. This Indian had struck our vulnerable spot, unveiled a truth to which we are blind."[18]

So impressed is Jung with the superiority of the passive, detached Indian over the striving, agitated white that he comes to attribute all the individuating qualities of American culture to the Indians. As a biographer tells it:

After his stay with the Pueblo Indians, Jung was even more convinced than before of the profound imprint of the American Indian upon the collective mind of America. Jung noted that Americans were obsessed, to an unusual degree, by the pursuit of a sort of Heroic Ideal, and that this heroic attitude, with its primitive reckless features, had been largely acquired through identification with the Red Man. Jung cited American sports, the "toughest" in the world, from which the idea of play had almost disappeared, as a prime example of this heroic stance. He stressed the parallels between the initiation ceremonies of American college fraternities and those of Indian tribes. He was struck by the profusion of secret societies of every description, from the Ku Klux Klan to the Knights of Columbus, and by the resemblance of their rites to those of primitive mystery religions. And he did not fail to notice the analogy between the spiritual healing of Christian Science and the shamanistic practices of American Indians, observing that both, though unscientific, proved to be "pretty effective." He saw this "Indianization" of the American mind even tangibly mirrored in the skyline of New York or Chicago, with the "houses piling up to towers towards the centre," just like the pueblos of the southwestern Indians. "Without conscious imitation the American unconsciously fills out the spectral outline of the Red Man's mind and temperament."[19]

It does not take a particularly penetrating intellect to see the falsity of this kind of thinking. The aggressiveness of American athletes relates more readily to the aggressiveness of the early explorers, the violent and single-minded conquistadores, than to that of their victims, the Indians. There are secret societies with initiation ceremonies in every culture; Jung might have noticed them in Fascist Europe, for instance. Similarly, spiritual healing is found in every culture. And if urban Americans raise towers in their cities, it is because they are bodying forth the desires of their aggressive Renaissance forebears, not those of the Indians, the vast majority of whom lived in lodges and tents rather than in adobe skyscrapers. But Jung was not a very good observer in the first place or he would have noted the inaccuracy of the portrait that his Indian interlocutor drew for him and that started a chain of thought that led to a false idealization of Native Americans. For while it is true that some whites

have thin lips, sharp noses, and so on, it is inconceivable
that a Swiss who had spent much time in German-speaking
countries would not be aware that there are in the world a
great number of round, well-fed white faces bespeaking a
certain contentment and complacency (just as there are, no
doubt, a good many Indians with aquiline features).

When he comes to Oriental cultures, Jung is no better,
drawing the same kind of hard and fast (and thus false) distinctions:

> The mythic needs of the Occidental call for an
> evolutionary cosmogony with a beginning and a goal.
> The Occidental rebels against a cosmogony with a
> beginning and a mere end, just as he cannot accept
> the idea of a static, self-contained, eternal cycle
> of events. The Oriental, on the other hand, seems
> able to come to terms with this idea. Apparently
> there is no unanimous feeling about the nature of
> the world, any more than there is general agree-
> ment among contemporary astronomers on this ques-
> tion. To Western man, the meaninglessness of a
> merely static universe is unbearable. He must as-
> sume that it has meaning. The Oriental does not
> need to make this assumption; rather, he himself
> embodies it. Whereas the Occidental feels the need
> to complete the meaning of the world, the Oriental
> strives for the fulfillment of meaning in man, strip-
> ping the world and existence from himself (Bud-
> dha). [20]

Note the language used to describe the two types: the anxious
and overwrought Occidental "rebels against" and "cannot accept" the "meaninglessness" of a world whose meaning he
"feels the need to complete"; the smiling and self-contained
Oriental, on the other hand, "seems able to come to terms
with this idea" and, indeed, "he himself embodies it." Jung's
biographer gives the impression that he was irascible and
quarrelsome, and certainly this description, which on the
surface champions the Eastern cause, seems designed to an-
tagonize those Westerners who might resent Jung's unflatter-
ing portrait. With friends like these, what need has monism
of enemies?

Jung has been dealt with at some length here in order
to show how ostensibly sympathetic and well-meaning students
of philosophical systems can cloud the issue. And when a

thinker as renowned as Jung separates human thought into
two distinct hemispheres that never touch, the danger of misunderstanding is increased proportionately. As the discussion
of Western philosophy from Thales forward shows, monism
and dualism can be thought of as interrelated rather than opposed. A truly comprehensive study of the two viewpoints
would demonstrate their coexistence in all cultures at all
times in human history, but it will suffice here to examine
representative forms of monism, the less familiar viewpoint,
as it appears in different forms, particularly in the West.
Accordingly, while I shall begin with a look at Zen Buddhism,
one of the purest forms of monism, I shall give more time to
the "rational monism" of the Stoics and Epicureans (as opposed to the "irrational dualism" of Plato); to Christian monism; and, finally, to the monism implicit in Freudian psychology. I am assuming that my readers, like myself, are
dualists born and bred, and that by guiding them through these
manifestations of an unfamiliar philosophy rather than offering
only the dictionary definition given in the Preface, I shall
best prepare them for an appreciation of the remainder of the
book, which is devoted largely to literary expressions of monism in the West. If I seem overly casual about putting theo-
logians, philosophers, psychologists, and literary artists on
the same footing, I would ask my readers to bear in mind
that all of these seekers are involved in "the redefinition of
reality," a phrase to which I shall return at the close of the
chapter.

★

The ingrained hostility in the West toward Eastern thought is
for the most part due to abuses of Eastern practices by Westerners who are either stupid or venal or both. Kenneth Rexroth, himself a subtle exponent of Eastern thought and aesthetics, tells the following story:

> I have no use for hippy and beat Zen because it's
> essentially antinomianism. I was playing the Five
> Spot, a cafe in New York some years ago, and the
> chief beatnik was standing at the bar. We hadn't
> opened yet. And a court officer came in to serve
> this fellow with a summons for child support and
> alimony for his wife and child, both of whom had
> tuberculosis. When he was handed the summons he
> announced, "This doesn't mean anything to me, I'm
> a Zen buddhist." And he tore it up. The owner
> said, "I don't give a damn if you're Mary Baker

Eddy and a Christian Scientist. Get out of here."
That's what the kids all over the world have eaten
up: Buddhism means irresponsibility. Well, it so
happens that the Buddhist law for the layman in the
simplest Theravada sects has between 40 and 48
commandments, all of which include the Mosaic code
except sabbath and business about God. So to say,
"I'm a Buddhist, I don't believe in the Ten Commandments," is not Buddhism. Buddhism includes
the Ten Commandments and surpasses them. So I
think this stuff [hippy and beat Zen] is largely per-
nicious. 21

Unfortunately, "hippy and beat Zen" is the only kind most
Westerners know; the very words conjure up images of bongo-
thumping beatniks in sunglasses, ostensibly rebelling against
the workaday world while they live off of welfare payments
or money from home received on the sly. These misleading
images linger long past the historical period in which they
arose; they dishonored a venerable tradition then and continue
to do so today.

Because of this pervasive misinformation, perhaps the
best way to provide accurate information would be to list some
common objections to Zen Buddhism and then refute them.
First, if Zen thought (and Buddhist thought in general) is
monistic, then it must require the rejection of that dualism
that is the spice of Western life; after all, the creation and
satisfaction of appetites is a dualistic activity enjoyed to some
degree by all of us in this consumer society, no matter how
religious or philosophical our outlook. To refute this idea,
we need only return to the discussion earlier in this chapter
of the interrelatedness of monism and dualism. Though it
is true that Westerners ordinarily think in terms of opposites,
the Zen thinker believes, not in simple unity, but in the idea
that things are "one and not one" at the same time. You are
you, I am I, John is a man, Jane is a woman--the four of
us are not one. Yet we have our humanity in common, and
thus we are one, or, more accurately, we are "one and not
one" at the same time.

This is a profoundly satisfying realization, in its way.
To contemplate it for long is perhaps to understand why, as
discussed earlier, the Orient never really embarked on "that
reckless adventure of the mind" that is science. This is a
historical fact rather than a value judgment, of course. Applied science is the ultimate dualism, since it seeks to man-

age and conquer real "foes." When such foes include disease
and pollution, then the dualists who rout them are to be ap-
plauded. This is common sense. And despite its reputation
for flightiness and irresponsibility, Zen is nothing if not commonsensical. The realization that disparate beings are "one
and not one" is not simplistic in nature, but it requires no
training, no sophisticated analytical tools--only common sense.

A second objection to Buddhism is that it replaces a
Judeo-Christian dualistic cosmology, which is questionable to
many already, with one that is even more complex. At least
with God and the Devil you know where you stand. To refute
this idea, we need to consider the origin of Buddhism. At
the time that the Buddha was traveling the length of India and
preaching his new doctrine, the predominant religious system
was Brahmanism. [22] According to this system, the universe
has as its supreme being the Brahman, a pantheistic principle
of reality to which Emerson alluded in his references to the
"Oversoul." There is some of this absolute quality in each
individual, in the form of the atman, a Sanskrit word meaning both "self" and "universal self" and corresponding to our
idea of "soul." (In Brahmanism, as in Christianity, this
"soul" is seen as permanent and unchanging, a point of dispute in Buddhism.) Anyone who wished to experience the ful-
fillment that comes with the uniting of the atman with the
Brahman was obliged to practice a complex mental and physical discipline called yoga. As with Zen, "yoga" is a word
that has certain ludicrous connotations in the West, and while
it may conjure up visions of leotard-clad housewives sitting
in painful positions, the word itself means (in Sanskrit) "to
unite or be yoked with God." Naturally enough, this yoking
process in Brahmanism was overseen by a priestly class who
alone understood the secrets of the universe.

But the Buddha disputed their authority. According
to his teachings, there was neither universal Oversoul nor
individual soul. Thus, enlightenment, far from consisting of
merging with the godhead, consists of realizing that there
is nothing with which to merge. Freed from the necessity
of attaining union with this godhead, the individual is able to
concentrate on tasks that are simpler, more easily accomplished, and just as worthy. The goal of Buddhism is to
make life bearable and, if possible, blissful. Buddhism has
evolved into a complex system of thought (witness Kenneth
Rexroth's mention of the numerous commandments adhered
to by Theravada Buddhists), but the Zen school retains the
original simplicity that the Buddha espoused when he turned
away from Brahmanism.

Probably the most unique aspect of Zen is its indifference to doctrine. The emphasis is on practice rather than philosophical understanding. In fact, the word "Zen" derives from a Sanskrit term meaning "concentrated contemplation," or, more accurately, "meditation." And meditation is a physical activity first and foremost. The goal is to attain certain desirable mental and emotional states, but these are attained only if one is sitting comfortably and without distraction. Thus meditation--and Zen itself--is all practice, no theory. [23]

Exponents of Zen are fond of emphasizing its ordinary nature. There is nothing extraordinary about it; Zen consists of everyday activity, though everyday activity conducted mindfully rather than blindly (hence one occasionally sees poems with titles like "The Zen of Housework," by the American poet Al Zolynas). In Zen Mind, Beginner's Mind, Shunryu Suzuki points out that while all of us are moved whenever we pass by a monastery or convent toward the evening and hear the bells ring and the doves coo as the cloistered religious go through their centuries-old rituals, to the religious themselves it is a matter of business as usual. So far from being complex, the Zen form of Buddhism is the simplest of any religion or philosophy because it is not a religion or a philosophy at all but a practice. The famous Zen riddle asks, "What did the shoemaker do after he attained enlightenment?" The answer is, "He went on making shoes." Another kind of shoemaker would be expected to profit from his new state, to use it in order to take over the shoe factory, perhaps, or to abandon shoemaking altogether in order to market low-cost enlightenment techniques (through a nationwide network of franchise outlets, no doubt). But the Zen shoemaker goes on doing what he always did, happy that he is no longer tortured by the lure of ever-greater goals, happy to be ordinary.

A third objection to Zen, and the strongest in this rational culture of ours, is that Zen thrives on paradox--it does not make sense. The Judeo-Christian system tells us what to do, even if we choose not to do it. But how do the celebrated koans help? What impact can an unanswerable question like "What is the sound of one hand clapping?" have on the moral choices we must make daily? The justification of these paradoxes is that they remind us that simple answers, ones we can be sure of, do not suffice. There is no answer to "What is the sound of one hand clapping?" because sometimes there is no answer. A corollary to this idea is that sometimes there is no question and that perhaps we make

more choices than we have to.  Again, mindfulness is emphasized over a set of rules to be followed blindly.

An objection to the paradoxical nature of Zen teachings
is somewhat hypocritical unless we are contrasting the koans
with Western modes of expression no more sophisticated than,
say, a stop sign.  After all, the story of Western art, at
least in this century, is the story of nonrepresentation, of
Finnegans Wake, Guernica, and Waiting for Godot.  To think
of such works as these in relation to the paradoxes of Zen is
to realize the existence of a tradition of illogic that, like the
tradition of monism and quietism itself, is no less real simply because it is subordinate to other, more obvious traditions.
Thomas Hoover reminds us that

> the apparent nonsense and illogic of Zen parables
> established the limitations of language long before
> the theater of the absurd decided to ridicule our
> modern doublespeak; indeed, our new-found skepti-
> cism about language as a medium for communica-
> tion was a commonplace to Japanese artists who
> created both a drama (the Nō) and a poetry (the
> Haiku) that neatly circumvent reliance on mere
> words for expression. [24]

Another Zen paradox is, "If you meet the Buddha on
the road, kill him."  When you think you are the most certain, you are farthest from the truth--that is, you have accepted a simple certainty in place of the hard-won mindfulness that is the result of proper meditation.  The person
who says, "I am enlightened!" is the most benighted of per-
sons, the most self-deceived.  The most advanced Zen adept
is not an expert but a beginner, because to the beginner there
are many possibilities, to the expert few.  "Zen mind" and
"beginner's mind" are synonymous phrases.

A final paradox of Zen can be expressed this way:
"We should find perfect existence through imperfect existence."
When we have strong desires and we manage to fulfill them,
we experience what seems to be perfection, at least for a
time.  But then we discover that the object of our desire is
imperfect or inadequate in ways that we were not able to
foresee--thus, the Zen emphasis on detachment.  If to obtain
what we desire is perfect, then to regard it from a distance
is imperfect, yet it is permanent--that which we renounce we
have forever, while that which we obtain we have only temporarily, since the more we examine it the more we see it
change.  Hence, perfection through imperfection.

Perhaps the best illustration of this idea for a Westerner involves our Christmas experiences. We see the decorations go up in the stores, we hear carols on the radio, we buy and trim a tree, we watch as the gaily wrapped packages mount in ever higher stacks, we feel our own anticipation swell and feed off the rising anticipations of others, until the day comes and we open our gifts: a tie, a pen-and-pencil set, some bookends. Of course, we do not actually grieve, and in fact we are quietly pleased that our loved ones thought of us at all. Still, and even though we were never very firm about what we wanted in the first place, what we actually got was decidedly less. By contrast, most of us have pleasant memories of past Christmases as well as active hopes for wonderful Christmases in the future. These Christmases of the imagination, the ones we never had (at least not quite as we remember them) as well as the ones we never will have (at least not quite as we foresee them) are the only ones that are perfect. The proof that this is a valid argument lies in the fact that, despite our consistent disappointment every December 25, we continue to view the holiday season fondly. Were it not for our intuitive grasp of the benign imperfection of Christmas, the already-high rate of holiday suicides would be even worse.

If Westerners at large remain skeptical of Zen, one group at least seems more receptive than it has been in decades past, and it is a group that one might expect to offer the most vociferous opposition. I refer to the scientific community. Part of this new tolerance is due to the advent of quantum mechanics and the concomitant realization that logic has its limits, that measurement is sometimes impossible, that certainty is often unattainable. Newtonian physics is still applicable, but only to the macroscopic universe; quantum mechanics, which resulted from a study of the microscopic or subatomic realm, is necessary to complement the older methods. [25] If we were to allow a gram of radium to sit for sixteen hundred years, for example, we would find that its mass has diminished by half. This is predictable and in keeping with Newtonian physics. But it is impossible to know which of the radium atoms are going to disintegrate and which are not; there is no physical law governing this selection, even though there is a physical law that predicts with certainty the disintegration of precisely half of the atoms. [26] In this way, the different outlooks of Newtonian physics and quantum mechanics provide us with a complete picture of the world.

The original subatomic scientists could not have

realized that their findings simply confirmed a fundamental if
only recently examined aspect of the human brain, but this
is the case, and it brings us to another development that accounts for increasing scientific tolerance of Buddhist illogic.
I refer to the comparatively recent discovery that the brain
has two quite different sections. [27]  The left hemisphere gov-
erns our abilities to analyze and dissect; it is linked with the
right-hand side of our bodies.  The right hemisphere is the
seat of intuition and nonverbal perception; it controls the side
that is "sinister" (French sinistre, "left") and accounts for
our suspicion of the left-handed.  Despite Thales' early and
ill-fated attempt to explain the world holistically ("Everything
is really water"), Western thinkers have maintained an insistence on the superiority of the left hemisphere, the analytical one.  There are exceptions, of course.  In fact, this
book is about those exceptions.  But the point is that logic
is the single most characteristic quality of Western philosophy.
By contrast, Eastern philosophy in general and Zen Buddhism
in particular advance the opposite point of view.  In doing so,
they simply confirm what scientists are beginning to understand:  that there are ways to experience reality that are not
logical and analytical yet that are necessary for a total view.

I might have concluded my brief survey of monistic
practices and outlooks with these remarks on Zen Buddhism,
but I wanted to put them first in order to make it absolutely
clear that I am not following the example of Jung and other
ostensibly sympathetic Western thinkers who discover at last
an Eastern outlook "superior" to the one that has always but-
tered their bread.  Too, I wanted to begin with Zen in order
to start with a pure form of monism, one that is necessarily
hard to understand because it is not touched by terms and
personalities familiar to us, ones to which we might give un-
due importance in order to keep from floundering in a sea of
illogic.  If the reader has followed the commentary to this
point, however, it should be relatively easy to discern examples of monism where we have not seen them before.  One
such example is the "rational monism" of the Stoic and Epicurean philosophers.

To begin to understand this "rational monism," we
must look first at the "irrational dualism" of Plato.  The
phrase "irrational dualism," especially when it comes after a
sympathetic discussion of Zen Buddhism, is enough to raise
the blood pressure of any logic-lover.  But the key word "irrational" is not used here in a pejorative way.  It means
simply "not established by the process of reason."  The idea

of Plato's irrationality becomes clear when we consider Plato's scheme of things.  As I discussed earlier in this chapter, there is a distinction in Platonic thinking between the apparitional world and the real world.  As Whitney J. Oates puts it,

> Plato recognized basically two modes of being, one the phenomenal realm, the world of "sights and sounds" as he described it, and the other the realm of the ideas or forms, non-spatial, non-temporal entities, which exist "apart" from the realm of phenomena.  The phenomenal world is characterized as impermanent, fraught with changes--things continually come into being and pass out of being, whereas the ideal realm is the realm of permanence and timelessness.  Reality in the full sense is to be found only in the realm of ideas" [emphasis mine]. 28

Plato's dualism is at the heart of many a worthy philosophical and religious system, including mainstream Christianity and its promise of a better life hereafter--literally, the only real life.  Regardless of one's personal feelings on the subject, however, the fact remains that such a division between worlds is predicated more on hope and exalted feeling than on empirical evidence.

By contrast, Stoic and Epicurean thought is marked by "rational monism."  The Stoics, says Oates, "insisted that any theory that the cosmos was radically dualistic was not tenable.  The universe, if it is of any value at all, must be self-sufficient; hence if self-sufficient, it must be untainted with dualism, and therefore monistic."29  Just as Oates does not use the term "irrational" in a pejorative way above, so he does not use "rational" here as a term of praise.  In fact, "rational" is, here, virtually synonymous with "materialistic."  This is another term that we must strip of its judgmental connotation if we are to use it accurately.  In the present context, to say that we are "materialists" does not mean that we have exaggerated desires for bigger cars, fancier houses, and better-looking mates.  It means simply that we apprehend a material world through our rational, everyday senses (such an understanding of the world, it will be recalled, is at the heart of Zen Buddhism and can be said to exist at the heart of all "commonsensical" or nonidealistic philosophies).  This world we apprehend is monistic in nature.  It is one piece--our senses tell us that, just as they tell us that the opposite of this world, a more real world, such as Plato's realm of ideas or the Christian heaven, does not exist. Or if it does, its existence will have to be established through inspiration or desire. It will have to be felt or wished into existence, because our rational, everyday minds tell us there is no such world.

The commonsense nature of these observations notwithstanding, monism continues to be looked at disdainfully in most quarters here in the West. This is to be expected. Dualism is the striving -ism that longs to conquer; monism is the self-sufficient -ism that cannot be bothered with conflict, and therefore it is fated to lose all conflicts. Sadly, dualism is not content with victory but insists on libeling its defeated rival. Thus, "various philosophers and critics in the history of Western European thought have made the mistake of supposing that the materialistic monism of Epicurus is an ignoble philosophy." (In the city in which this book is being written, there is a restaurant group managed by Epicurean Associates, Inc., the idea being that Epicureanism is synonymous with rich food, strong drink, gay surroundings, and the high life in general.) But "it can be confidently asserted that such is not the case," says Oates, "for what Epicurus sought primarily to do was to rid men from certain besetting fears which tainted their lives, namely the fear of the gods which led to superstitious enormities, and fear of death with all its concomitants." Interestingly, the goal of Epicurus sounds much like that of the Buddha when he sought to dissociate his audiences from the polytheistic complexities of Brahmanism. Epicurus wanted to convince his listeners that everything consisted of what Oates calls "atoms and void," that is, matter and space. In other words, there are no ghostly gods, no fourth-dimensional afterworlds. Once rid of these "certain besetting fears," the Epicurean convert is able "to achieve peace of mind--inner calm and security-- which is his final desideratum, the best of pleasures." And with respect to pleasure, Oates points out that Epicurus "urges a careful discrimination among the several pleasures and categorically rejects such pleasures as may be momentarily intense but which are followed by attendant pain." Rather than being a sybarite, the Epicurean is one who "argues for the principle of the mean, or moderation, the joys that accrue from friendship, and the advantages of living a simple life." Indeed, the true Epicurean is liable to withdraw from active participation in life altogether--the best known of Epicurus' maxims, the famous Fragment 86, says simply, "Live unknown." Again, the parallel with what we know of Zen could hardly be stronger. "Only by a rigorous development and discipline of the will can these precepts be followed," observes Oates, and therefore "one must conclude that, far from being an ignoble philosophy, Epicureanism is an enlightened creed." Given "its materialistic limits," Epicureanism is "as enlightened as it could possibly be."[30]

Though I shall make a distinction between the two philosophies shortly, it must be said that as we move from Epicureanism to Stoicism, we stay within the realm of rational and materialistic philosophies as opposed to irrational and idealistic ones, such as Platonism and Christianity (again, with the understanding that these adjectives are meant to be descriptive and not judgmental). Certainly, the starting point for the two philosophies is the same: like Epicurus, the Stoic Epictetus is aware that human beings are made hesitant and unhappy by "certain besetting fears," and thus his goal is to dispel those fears. Oates points out that in common with the other Stoics, Epictetus "holds up internal calm and peace of mind as that which is finally to be desired." Such peace of mind is attained only by way of the mindfulness that the Buddhists espouse, and for similar reasons. Crucial to this mindfulness is "the proper use of impressions, which involves the keen discrimination between things in our power and those not in our power."[31] Marcus Aurelius, Epictetus' disciple, says this:

> Remember to retire into this little territory of thine own, and above all, do not distract or strain thyself, but be free, and look at things as a man, as a human being, as a citizen, as a mortal. But among the things readiest to thy hand to which thou shalt turn, let there be these, which are two. One is that things do not touch the soul, for they are external and remain immovable; but our perturbations come only from the opinion which is within. The other is that all these things, which thou seest, change immediately and will no longer be; and constantly bear in mind how many of these changes thou hast already witnessed.[32]

Of course, as with Zen, Epicureanism, and other philosophies that appear to emphasize passivity and the lack of a need for exertion, in Stoicism as well the price of freedom is constant and strenuous self-discipline.

While these remarks are intended to point out some

of the similarities shared by different monistic outlooks, it would be a mistake to assume that an attempt is being made to equate any of them, especially Epicureanism and Stoicism. Indeed, to mention these two philosophies in the same breath is paradoxical. Oates reminds us that Epicureanism recommends ('an ascetic withdrawal from the world, a retirement 'into the Garden,' in order to gain peace.') On the other hand, the Stoic system "maintains that the peace must be found in the midst of the world's confusions, for after all, all men are brothers."[33] But a paradox is not a contradiction. Stoicism and Epicureanism do not cancel each other out; to subscribe to one philosophy is not to forswear the other. The behavior of no one is fixed, and it is not only understandable but desirable to move between one pattern of behavior and another, complementary pattern. Perhaps a studied alternation between the private self-cultivation of the Epicureans and the disciplined public involvement of the Stoics will result in the most useful and happy life for most people. Besides, the two systems have at least this much in common: (1) they stress inner peace and calm, and (2) their foundations are rational and material.

It is important to emphasize this last point, since it is easy to associate monism with drugs, trances, and so on, and to think of it as an emotional and mystical phenomenon. The ghosts of Beatnik Zen and pop guruism will haunt us for some time to come. But more often than not, modern interpreters of monistic philosophies emphasize their practical, rational nature. In an essay on "The Keystones of Senecan Philosophy," which is a Stoic philosophy, Anna Lydia Motto describes the fundamental importance of rationalism in this way:

> The follies, errors, and sins of men spring from unreason; men grasp the faulty notion of the good, fostered by a greedy desire for external things that are dependent on Fortune.... [However], happiness is not to be found in riches, power, or the pleasure of the senses--gifts of fortune that are flashy, fleeting, deceptive--but in the untainted and rational mind.... Man is capable of self-regulation, of attaining to wisdom. And the wise man will detach himself from fickle Fortune's material gifts. He must regard them, rather, as household furniture, lent to him, which can be capriciously withdrawn....
> Because man is self-determining, he does possess the capacity to change, to learn virtue and

wisdom. And once he has achieved independence of
the whims of chance, man has become wise, has become completely free and happy.... Free from dis-
quietude, the newly initiated wise man enjoys a liberty and serenity of mind that are unalterable.
Since his happiness is internally acquired, so it
can never be destroyed by external forces.... Naturally, the reformation that produces such tranquillity is man's own spark of divine reason. Any man
who grooms and nourishes his reason may secure
some degree of virtue. [34]

Our journey from less familiar outlooks (Zen Buddhism)
through more familiar ones (Epicureanism and Stoicism) now
finds us on the borders of one of the greatest philosophical
and religious systems of all: Christianity. Virtually no one
in the West is untouched by it. The atheist, if true to principle, must fight it constantly, and even the agnostic who
never gives a thought to Christianity has to deal everyday
with Christian politicians and schoolteachers. None of us
can enter a post office or make a bank deposit on Sunday,
and even the most irreligious of us looks forward to Christmas and Easter. The more we realize how Christianity
shapes our lives, the more we should want to know exactly
what Christianity is. And the more closely we examine that
question, the more we come to see that what we think of as
Christianity today is a comparatively narrow and specialized
system. Our lives could just as well be shaped by one of
the several alternative "Christianities" that vied for dominance against the mainstream Christianity that became the
leading social and political as well as religious force in the
West. That struggle for dominance is one of the truly interesting footnotes to history.

Several years ago, a book called The Gnostic Gospels
appeared. It made a decisive splash in the media, then disappeared from the view of all but a few Biblical scholars.
Written by a Barnard College scholar named Elaine Pagels,
The Gnostic Gospels strikes the reader as one book that
might be described by the terms that Melville applied to
Moby-Dick, a "wicked book," one "roasted in hellfire." It
is a wicked book because, like Moby-Dick, if it were to be
read properly, it would spell the end for the established order
as it exists today. As Norman O. Brown writes in Closing
Time:

I sometimes think I see that civilizations originate

> in the disclosure of some mystery, some secret;
> and expand with the progressive publication of their
> secret; and end in exhaustion when there is no longer
> any secret, when the mystery has been divulged,
> that is to say profaned.... And so there comes
> a time--I believe we are in such a time--when
> civilization has to be renewed by the discovery of
> new mysteries. 35

If mainstream Christianity is the mystery that gave rise to
an entire culture, the revelations of The Gnostic Gospels
could be the "new mystery" for which seers like Brown are
waiting.

The story of the discovery of this particular mystery
is more exciting than any fictional analog of it could possibly
be. In December 1945, some Arab brothers digging for fert-
ilizer near the town of Nag Hammadi in Egypt found a red
earthenware jar nearly a meter high. They hesitated to break
it for fear that a djinn might live inside. But on the assump-
tion that the jar was as likely to contain gold, one of the
brothers smashed it with his mattock and found that the jar
held thirteen papyrus books bound in leather. They took the
books home and put them by the oven. Their mother used a
number of the pages to start fires, and possibly all of the
books would have been burned had it not been for one of those
quirks of circumstance that seem almost necessary to impel
such events as these to public significance. A few weeks
after the discovery of the books, the brothers, who had been
involved in a blood feud of long standing, avenged their father's murder by committing a murder of their own. They
hacked the alleged assassin of their father with the mattocks
that had been used to dig up the jar; they ripped his heart
out and devoured it. Fearing that the police would find and
take the books while investigating the murder, the brothers
arranged for one or more of the books to be kept by the local priest. A history teacher saw a book, and word of their
existence spread, finally reaching Cairo. Officials of the
Egyptian government bought one of the leatherbound volumes
and confiscated another ten and a half, depositing them in the
Coptic Museum in Cairo. Part of another book was smuggled
out of the country and offered for sale; eventually it was
bought by the Jung Foundation in Zurich and examined by Professor Gilles Quispel, a distinguished historian of religion
from Utrecht. When Professor Quispel discovered that some
of the pages were missing, he flew to Cairo in the spring of
1955 to try to find them. He hurried to the Coptic Museum,

borrowed some photographs of the pages that had been taken earlier, and took them back to his hotel to translate them. Quispel was startled, then incredulous, when he saw that the first line read: "These are the secret words which the living Jesus spoke, and which the twin, Judas Thomas, wrote down."[36]

Further investigation showed that the books were Coptic translations, made about fifteen hundred years earlier, of still more ancient manuscripts. Just how old the originals were is hard to say. Quispel and others have suggested circa A.D. 140 as the date of the originals. Recently, however, another scholar has argued that the Nag Hammadi manuscripts contain references to traditions that date back to A.D. 50-100, meaning that the gnostic gospels may have been written at about the same time as or even earlier than the gospels of the New Testament, which are dated circa A.D. 60-110.

The general subject matter of the Nag Hammadi manuscripts is frequently the same as that of Matthew, Mark, Luke, and John, but the details are often strikingly different, even antithetical. One of the texts, The Gospel of Philip, reports:

> ... the companion of the [Savior is] Mary Magdalene. [But Christ loved] her more than [all] the disciples, and used to kiss her [often] on her [mouth]. The rest of [the disciples were offended].... They said to him, "Why do you love her more than all of us?" The Savior answered and said to them, "Why do I not love you as (I love) her?"[37]

The gnostic version of Genesis is told from the viewpoint of the serpent, who represents the principle of divine wisdom, and portrays God as a jealous and threatening being who wants to keep Adam and Eve from attaining knowledge. Another text with an Oriental-sounding title, Thunder, Perfect Mind, is a poem spoken by a female deity:

> For I am the first and the last.
> I am the honored one and the scorned one.
> I am the whore and the holy one.
> I am the wife and the virgin....
> I am the barren one,
>     and many are her sons....

> I am the silence that is incomprehensible....
> I am the utterance of my name. [38]

Many of the gnostic texts refer to both the Old and New Testaments, and the dramatis personae, principally Jesus and his disciples, are often the same as those of conventional scripture. According to the gnostics, the world is ruled by evil archons, among them the tyrannical Jehovah of the Old Testament, who is distinguished from the supreme being, the ineffable Fore-Father or Abyss. The mission of Jesus is to fan into flame the spark of divinity in everyone, while the archons want to keep humankind in subjugation. This world view leads to marked doctrinal differences between gnostics and mainstream Christians. Pagels notes three main distinctions:

(1) Mainstream Christians (and Jews as well) follow the Platonic lead in insisting that God is wholly other, whereas some gnostic texts say that the self and the divine are identical, that self-knowledge is knowledge of God. The Jesus of the gnostic texts ridicules the idea of a separate God and a separate Kingdom:

> "If those who lead you say to you, 'Look, the Kingdom is in the sky,' then the birds will arrive there before you. If they say to you, 'It is in the sea,' then, he says, the fish will arrive before you."

But the disciples persist in the belief that God and His Kingdom are distant:

> His disciples said to him, "When will ... the new world come?" He said to them, "What you look forward to has already come, but you do not recognize it...." His disciples said to him, "When will the Kingdom come?" [Jesus] said, "It will not come by waiting for it. It will not be a matter of saying 'Here it is' or 'There it is.' Rather, the Kingdom of the Father is spread upon the earth, and men do not see it."

In other words, the Kingdom is a state of transformed consciousness, not a literal place:

> Jesus saw infants being suckled. He said to his disciples, "These infants being suckled are like those who enter the Kingdom." They said to

him, "Shall we, then, as children, enter the Kingdom?" Jesus said to them, "When you make the
two one, and when you make the inside like the outside and the outside like the inside, and the above
like the below, and when you make the male and the
female one and the same ... then you will enter
[the Kingdom]."[38]

(2) Whereas the New Testament Jesus speaks of sin
and repentance, the gnostic Jesus speaks of illusion and en-
lightenment--as a Hindu or a Buddhist might, or, as Pagels
points out, as a modern psychotherapist might (I will return
to this comparison later in the chapter). Mainstream Christians see benevolent and malevolent forces as external, while
gnostics say that the psyche contains within itself the potential
for liberation or destruction. As Jesus says in the gnostic
Gospel of Thomas:

> "If you bring forth what is within you, what you
> bring forth will save you. If you do not bring forth
> what is within you, what you do not bring forth will
> destroy you."[39]

(3) Mainstream Christians believe that Jesus, like God,
is distinct from humanity, but the gnostics see him as an enlightened person, a teacher and a spiritual master. In this
sense, Jesus is like the Buddha or, as Pagels would have it,
like a psychotherapist, one who uses his authority in such a
way that his disciples will eventually outgrow it. The gnostic
Jesus says:

> "Whoever will drink from my mouth will become
> as I am, and I myself will become that person, and
> the things that are hidden will be revealed to him."

But just as the disciples could not grasp easily the idea of
an internal Kingdom, so they find it hard to accept the notion
of their autonomy (it is interesting to see how strongly the
gnostics emphasize not only the teachings of their Jesus but
also the difficulty that others, even the already-converted,
have in accepting these teachings):

> Jesus said to his disciples, "Compare me to
> someone and tell me whom I am like." Simon
> Peter said to him, "You are like a righteous angel."
> Matthew said to him, "You are like a wise philoso-
> pher." Thomas said to him, "Master, my mouth

> is wholly incapable of saying whom you are like."
> Jesus said, "I am not your master. Because you
> have drunk, you have become drunk from the bub-
> bling stream which I have measured out."

And again:

> When the disciples, expecting him to reveal secrets
> to them, ask Jesus, "Who is the one who seeks,
> [and who is the one who] reveals?" he answers that
> the one who seeks the truth--the disciple--is also
> the one who reveals it. Since Matthew persists in
> asking him questions, Jesus says that he does not
> know the answer himself, "nor have I heard about
> it, except from you."[40]

The gnostic texts that express these beliefs were only
part of numerous other gospels, "secret teachings, myths,
and poems attributed to Jesus and his disciples" that circu-
lated among Christians during the first two centuries following Christ's death.[41] But by A.D. 200, Christianity had become a hierarchy of bishops, priests, and deacons, and the
church of Rome began to take a leading role amidst the diversity and proliferation of sects. Nonconformist viewpoints
were dismissed as heresy. The church father Irenaeus insisted that heretics--that is, those who argued for Christian
teachings outside the New Testament--be expelled. When the
mainstream viewpoint became allied with the military establishment, sometime after Constantine converted to Christianity
in the fourth century, heresy became not only an inadvisable
but often a fatal enterprise.

Who were the authors of these exotic, paradoxical,
often sensuous texts? Gnosticism was a varied and widespread movement deriving from both Jewish and Christian
sources; possibly it contained elements of Iranian and Egyptian religions. There may have been influences from farther
east. Trade routes between the Greco-Roman world and the
Far East were opening up during the heyday of gnosticism
(A.D. 80-200); Buddhist missionaries were known to have pros-
elytized in Alexandria; and tradition has it that the disciple
Thomas, for whom one of the gnostic gospels is named, went
to India. Like mainstream Christianity, gnosticism is dualistic at base. But gnosticism may be taken as paradigmatic
of much of Western culture in that it is characterized by
monistic tendencies that are sometimes subtle, sometimes
glaring.

It is easy to imagine gnostic longings developing among Jews intrigued with the mystical aspects of Hellenistic philosophy and disillusioned with their own heritage. One of the texts, The Apocryphon of John, is clearly a reaction against Jewish scriptures in its repeated use of the phrase "and not as Moses said" (Moses was commonly thought to be the author of the first five books of the Old Testament). In fact, it is not difficult to see the gnostic account of the cosmos as an attempt to reconcile the two different and essentially contradictory halves of the Bible by depicting Jehovah as a malevolent deity and Jesus as His foe rather than His assistant. At least this interpretation will appeal to those readers who have difficulty reconciling a relationship between an angry, selfish Father and a loving, self-sacrificial Son, which is what we are left with if we take the Old and New Testaments as a single, seamless document.

What is clear is that today traditional Christianity is based on a small number of scriptures that were selected from a larger number. The question is, who did the selecting, and why did they choose the texts that now make up what we call the Bible? An examination of one major difference between gnosticism and orthodox Christianity may lead to the answer to this question. For whereas the gnostics deny the resurrection of Jesus after the Crucifixion, mainstream Christians not only insist upon the miraculous reappearance but also make it the central belief of their faith. The importance of the resurrection lies in its necessity for the direct transmission of authority from Jesus to the apostles and from them to the anointed clergy of the Christian hierarchy. What the orthodox are saying to the dissenters, in effect, is this: while you were out, Jesus came back from the dead and put us in charge.

Giambattista Vico wrote of the tendency of rulers to keep the gods to themselves. According to him,

> the heroes or nobles, by a certain nature of theirs which they believed to be of divine origin, were led to say that the gods belonged to them, and consequently that the auspices of the gods were theirs also. By means of the auspices they kept within their own orders all the public or private institutions of the heroic cities. [42]

An understanding of this alliance between religious and political power leads to a reconsideration of history, not the

least of which is one's own personal experience. As a child,
I remember reciting the Apostles' Creed, uncomprehending yet
happy in the knowledge that I was saying a prayer and thereby
pleasing God. A knowledge of early church history makes it
clear, however, that if the Apostles' Creed is a prayer, it
is just as much a pledge of allegiance, not to God but to His
self-appointed spokesmen.

In a sense, the gnostics got what they asked for. Their
claim to an esoteric gnosis (Greek "knowledge") superior to
that of any other group is sufficient reason to think that many
of the gnostics must have been not only doctrinally and polit-
ically but also personally unbearable. The title of another
book on gnosticism, John Dart's The Laughing Savior,[43] hints
at the theme of mocking laughter that runs throughout the
gospels: Eve laughs at the archons who rape her likeness,
Jesus laughs at his persecutors as they pound nails into his
abandoned physical self. Even the most saintly of mortals
do not care to be mocked, and it is little wonder that the
orthodox found ways to silence these mirthful heretics. Besides, who would want to replace the New Testament's gentle
reason with the gnostic gospels' murkiness and lack of system? ("Every day everyone of them invents something new,"
complained Irenaeus of the gnostic Valentinus and his followers.[44])

If there is to be regret, it should not be over the
failure of gnosticism to supplant mainstream Christianity but
over the failure of the two outlooks to coexist in some fruit-
ful way. They are opposed, but only on the political level.
For as these comments have shown repeatedly, monism from
Thales forward is inclusive of dualism. So just as everything
is really water, and just as the world is one and not one at
the same time, so it is possible for the gnostics to see the
world in terms of a conflict between good and evil, as do
orthodox Christians, yet see that conflict as subject to the
transformations of mind. The emphasis in the New Testament is on the teachings of Jesus, which, like the doctrines
of Jefferson and Franklin, are laudable, even though they
sometimes seem neglectful of humanity's nastier tendencies.
(Randall Jarrell once wrote: "Most of us know, now, that
Rousseau was wrong; that man, when you knock his chains
off, sets up the death camps."[45]) The gnostic gospels emphasize a hard-bought awareness as the chief desideratum
rather than right behavior. The gnostics seem to be saying
that we are all born dualists, that we cannot help but see the
world in terms of conflict, but that if we discipline ourselves,

we will come to see that the conflict is within rather than
without.  And that means that we ourselves have the solution
to the conflict as well.

The gnostics were not the only ones to believe that
inner peace is worthier of contemplation than outer conflict.
At about the same time that Zen Buddhist monks were seeking
their ordinary selves in the East, a group of Christian monks
were doing something very similar half a world away, in the
Egyptian desert.  Commonly called the Desert Fathers, these
monks had the advantage over the gnostics of not posing a direct political threat to mainstream Christianity.  They were
thus allowed to pursue their ways unmolested, and the record
of their daily lives is an impressive example of monism func-
tioning in a dualistic world.  Their history comes down to us
through the Verba Seniorum, sayings transmitted orally in
Coptic before they were recorded in Syriac, Greek, and
Latin. 46  These Verba deal with every subject under the sun:
meditation, sin, diet, the temptations of the flesh, monastic
rules and regulations, the threat of robbery (apparently the
monks were not the only ones to flee to the desert for self-
betterment, and often the Verba give the impression that there
was a rough character hiding behind every rock).  Collec-
tively, though, the Verba Seniorum deal with striving for
purity of heart, a clear, unobstructed vision of the true state
of the world, an intuitive grasp of one's inner reality as an-
chored, or rather lost, in God through Christ.

The fruit of this striving was quies, or "rest."  Decidedly, this did not mean the rest of the body.  The Verba
give a picture of monks and hermits who are extremely active, and some of the sayings jibe rather pointedly at those
holy fathers who did not leaven their meditation with sufficient
manual labor.  And certainly, the quies has nothing to do with
fixation of the exalted spirit upon some point or summit of
light.  For the most part, the Desert Fathers were not ec-
statics.  Those who were left behind some strange and misleading stories to confuse the issue.  For the "rest" that
these monks sought was simply the sanity and poise of a being that no longer has to look at itself because it is carried
away by the perfection of freedom that is in it.  And carried where?  Wherever Love itself, or the Divine Spirit,
sees fit to go.

Rest, then, was a kind of simple nowhereness and no-
mindedness that had lost all preoccupation with a false or
limited self.  According to Thomas Merton's understanding

of it, to the Desert Fathers the true self was not an entity
but a state, the state of quies or rest, of "sanity and poise,"
that is no different from the same state as achieved by anyone else. [47]  It is the state of the world at rest, a state
evoked perhaps more often than we remember in the New
Testament in such lines, for example, as these:  "Consider
the lilies of the field, how they grow; they toil not, neither
do they spin" (Matthew 7:28).

Those who have not this authentic inner peace, say
the Desert Fathers, are at the mercy of a false or limited
self that compels them to toil and spin in a world made inauthentic by ignorance and lack of awareness.  Properly seen,
the idea of original sin is nothing more than this lack of
awareness.  Original sin is no one's fault, not even Adam's;
it is simply the state into which we are born and from which
we can extract ourselves only through the kind of discipline
practiced by the Desert Fathers.  In Zen and the Birds of
Appetite Merton writes:

> Buddhism and Biblical Christianity agree in their
> view of man's present condition.  Both are aware
> that man is somehow not in his right relation to the
> world and to things in it, or rather, to be more
> exact, they see that man bears in himself a mys-
> terious tendency to falsify that relation, and to
> spend a great deal of energy in justifying the false
> view he takes of his world and of his place in it.
> This falsification is what Buddhists call Avidya.
> Avidya, usually translated "ignorance," is the root
> of all evil and suffering because it places man in
> an equivocal, in fact impossible position.  It is an
> invincible error concerning the very nature of re-
> ality and man himself.  It is a disposition to treat
> the ego as an absolute and central reality and to
> refer all things to it as objects of desire or of re-
> pulsion.  Christianity attributes this view of man
> and of reality to "original sin. "[48]

Thus, original sin is not an arbitrary stigma but a "basic
inauthenticity, a kind of predisposition to bad faith in our
understanding of ourselves and of the world. "[49]  We inherit
an inauthentic self, one that separates us from the world and
from our true selves.  "What can we gain by sailing to the
moon if we are not able to cross the abyss that separates us
from ourselves?" asks Merton.  "This is the most important
of all voyages of discovery, and without it all the rest are

not only useless but disastrous." (Melville, whom we shall examine in the next chapter, tells us that "in the soul of man there lies one insular Tahiti, full of peace and joy, but encompassed by all the horrors of the half known life. God keep thee! Push not off from that isle, thou canst never return!"[50]) To Merton, the great travelers and colonizers of the Renaissance were men who sailed to other lands because their desire to travel could not be gratified by interior journeys, ones they were incapable of making. "In subjugating primitive worlds they only imposed on them, with the force of cannons, their own confusion and alienation."[51]

The Renaissance travelers and colonizers were extraordinary people, whereas the Desert Fathers, like Zen Buddhists, insisted on remaining human and "ordinary." According to Merton, this seems to be a paradox (that is, it is a paradox for a Christian, for one of "ours"; who is to know what is ordinary to a Buddhist?). Yet it is a crucial paradox.

> If we reflect a moment, we will see that to fly into the desert in order to be extraordinary is only to carry the world with you as an implicit standard of comparison. The result would be nothing but self-contemplation, and self-comparison with the negative standard of the world one had abandoned. Some of the monks of the Desert did this, as a matter of fact: and the only fruit of their trouble was that they went out of their heads. The simple men who lived their lives out to a good old age among the rocks and sands only did so because they had come into the desert to be themselves, their ordinary selves, and to forget a world that divided them from themselves. There can be no other valid reason for seeking solitude or for leaving the world.

When the Buddha was known as Sakyamuni (which means "Sage of the Sakyas," the clan from which he came), he said that self-realization is the greatest contribution one can make to society. This is why, even after he became the Enlightened One, he never involved himself in social justice, far less government.[52] So it was with the Desert Fathers. "To leave the world, is, in fact, to help save it in saving oneself. This is the final point," says Merton, "and it is an important one."[53]

★

Zen Buddhism, Epicureanism, Stoicism, gnosticism, desert
monasticism--how alien seem these arcane practices and outlooks, these esoteric -isms, to a writer who sits at an elec-
tric typewriter, is dressed in synthetic fabrics, is bathed in
fluorescent light.  Readers, too, will feel a sense of remove,
dependent as they are on electronic media, sophisticated
methods of conveyance, and all the other necessities of a
highly technological age.  Yet there is one thought system,
highly monistic in both conception and practice, that is not
only more revolutionary in its impact than any of those listed
above but also thoroughly contemporary and instantly familiar
to the reader.  I refer to the science of psychoanalysis.
Ernest Jones, Freud's biographer and a distinguished psychoanalyst in his own right, has written:

> The effect that psychoanalysis has had upon the
> life of the West is incalculable.  Beginning as a
> theory of certain illnesses of the mind, it went on
> to become a radically new and momentous theory of
> the mind itself.  Of the intellectual disciplines that
> have to do with the nature and destiny of mankind,
> there is none that has not responded to the force
> of this theory. [54]

Freud himself said there were three major revolutions:  the
revolution of Copernicus, which showed that the earth was
not the center of the universe; the revolution of Darwin, which
showed that man was not a unique creation; and the psychoanalytic revolution, which showed that man is not even master
in his own house.

    Properly understood, Freud is as much a philosopher
as he is a scientist.  Certainly, his work advanced "the cultural process of the redefinition of reality that in settled
periods of history is mainly the business of artists and philosophers, but that in the present dark times crucially involves those philosophers in spite of themselves--psychologists
and madmen."[55]  Pursuing the same idea in greater detail,
Freud's interpreter Norman O. Brown says that "the special
contribution of psychoanalysis is to trace religious and philosophic problems to their roots in the concrete human body."[56]
These problems are the ones that have always plagued what
Brown calls " 'dialectical' dreamers," namely, "psychoana-
lysts, political idealists, mystics, poets, philosophers."[57]
The problem for all of these dialectical dreamers is the
same.  It is that "mankind, in all its restless striving and
progress, has no idea of what it really wants.  Freud was

right," says Brown, "our real desires are unconscious."[58]
And if we are not conscious of our real desires, how can we
hope to obtain satisfaction? "Mankind today is still making
history without having any conscious idea of what it really
wants or under what conditions it would stop being unhappy;
in fact what it is doing seems to be making itself more unhappy and calling that unhappiness progress."[59]

As we have seen, Thomas Merton explains original
sin as inauthenticity--we are born into a state of original sin
when we are born into this inauthentic world. Freud's idea
is similar, although he would say that we are born into a
world of repression, one in which our unconscious desires
are schooled away so thoroughly that eventually we end up
schooling them away ourselves and then passing the lesson
on to the next generation. A particularly vivid expression
of this idea is Kenneth Rexroth's assertion that we are born
into a world covered by the Social Lie, the lie that begins at
home with Mommy telling the children that Daddy never mas-
turbated. [60] The idea that we live in a world of inauthenticity
or repression seems mild in contrast to Rexroth's belief that
we live in a world of lies.

> Remember again when you were a child. You
> thought that some day you would grow up and find
> a world of real adults--the people who really made
> things run--and understood how and why things ran.
> People like the Martian aristocrats in science fic-
> tion. Your father and mother were pretty silly,
> and the other grownups were even worse--but some-
> where, some day, you'd find the real grownups and
> possibly even be admitted to their ranks. Then,
> as the years went on, you learned, through more
> or less bitter experience, that there aren't, and
> never have been, any such people, anywhere. Life
> is just a mess, full of tall children, grown stupider,
> less alert, and resilient, and nobody knows what
> makes it go--as a whole, or any part of it. But
> nobody ever tells. [61]

Of course, people do tell--the dialectical dreamers do, and,
as we shall see, the poets and novelists discussed in the
remaining chapters of this book are concerned precisely with
"more or less bitter experience." The intent of Freud was
to penetrate the forest of lies that we tolerate, even perpetuate. Is he less of a philosopher than any of the others named
thus far? When Ernest Jones asked Freud how much philos-

ophy he had read, the reply was: "Very little. As a young
man I felt a strong attraction toward speculation and ruthlessly
checked it."[62] This remark is sometimes taken at face value
to mean that Freud thought of himself as nothing more than a
gifted scientist, an exceptional sort of mind doctor. Yet no
one questions the value of self-definitions more than Freud
does. And we know that he enrolled in a philosophy seminar
at the University of Vienna in the winter term of 1874-75;
that he continued in the same course the following term and
added one in Aristotle's logic; that he alleviated the boredom
of military service by translating a John Stuart Mill essay on
Plato; that he had enough confidence to write a general introduction, a "Philosophical A. B. C.," for his fiancée; that "in
the heady days of 1896, when he was piling discovery on discovery, he triumphantly told [his confidant Wilhelm] Fliess
in several letters that he was returning, by a circuitous route,
to his first ambition, to do original work in philosophy."[63]
Evidently, Freud's disdain for the philosopher's role is ex-
pressive of his distrust of speculation at the expense of clin-
ical evidence, an understandable reaction if we consider the
speculative nature of psychology both before and during Freud's
life, when the workings of the human mind were gauged largely
by what was thought of as "common sense" heavily leavened
with a Calvinistic morality. What we condemn we cannot always avoid, however. Jones notes that one of the hallmarks
of Freud's personality was a "fight between scientific discipline and philosophical speculation."[64] The degree to which
speculation triumphed can be seen in the extent to which
Freud is considered a philosopher by others. Jones notes,
for instance, that in Freud's own lifetime "the University of
London, in combination with the Jewish Historical Society,
arranged a series of lectures on five Jewish philosophers:
Philo, Maimonides, Spinoza, Freud, and Einstein."[65] Most
important of all is Freud's tendency to describe his desires
and accomplishments in philosophical language, his abhor-
rence of "philosophical speculation" notwithstanding. Jones
writes that he "can recall as far back as in 1910 [Freud's]
expressing the wish with a sigh that he could retire from medical practice and devote himself to the unraveling of cultural
and historical problems--ultimately the great problem of how
man came to be what he is."[66]

Freud's relation to psychoanalysis is a unique one in
cultural history. As Jones says, Freud was "not only the
one man who originated the science but also the one man who
brought it to maturity."[67] Yet, although we are accustomed
to thinking of Freud as an embattled truthseeker, which he

was, we must also recognize that his work took place within a context of support as well. Possibly the most representative pre-Freudian figure, as well as one who has discernible connections with some of the purer forms of monism as discussed above, is Schopenhauer. Whether or not he had an actual "addiction to Buddhism," as his biographer V. J. Mc-Gill asserts,[68] Schopenhauer had a sense of the relative insignificance of causality that would have done honor equally to a Zen sage or to Sigmund Freud.

> It was only in the eighteenth century that, in the wake of the Newtonian revolution, causality was enthroned as the absolute ruler of matter and mind-- only to be dethroned in the first decades of the twentieth, as a consequence of the revolution in physics. But even in the middle of the materialistic nineteenth century, that lone giant, Arthur Schopenhauer--who had a decisive influence on both Freud and Jung--proclaimed that physical causality was only one of the rulers of the world; the other was a metaphysical entity, a kind of universal consciousness, compared to which individual consciousness is as a dream compared to wakefulness.[69]

McGill reminds us that

> Schopenhauer's emphasis of the importance of unconscious sex motives, his pessimism and doctrine of the Will have led to important movements in modern psychology. Thanks to Schopenhauer and his disciple von Hartmann, these doctrines had already gained a currency in Europe long before Freud began to write and thus prepared for the wide reception of his extraordinary work.

Further, Schopenhauer held the opinion that

> the worst thing a man can do is to repress his quirks and idiosyncracies and never permit himself to speak of them, for such repression only strengthens the quirk into a fixed idea and conducts in the end to the madhouse. Here Schopenhauer anticipates, as in other cases, the theories of the modern psychoanalytic school.[70]

Like Freud's, Schopenhauer's genius lay in his dissatisfaction with the "common sense" view of things and his realization that real truths were not only different from apparent ones but also were frequently their opposites. Consider this passage from his essay "On the Suffering of the World":

> Just as a stream flows smoothly on as long as it
> encounters no obstruction, so the nature of man
> and animal is such that we never really notice or
> become conscious of what is agreeable to our will;
> if we are to notice something, our will has to have
> been thwarted, has to have experienced a shock of
> some kind. On the other hand, all that opposes,
> frustrates and resists our will, that is to say all
> that is unpleasant and painful, impresses itself upon
> us instantly, directly and with great clarity. Just
> as we are conscious not of the healthiness of our
> whole body but only of the little place where the
> shoe pinches, so we think not of the totality of our
> successful activities but of some insignificant trifle
> or other which continues to vex us. On this fact
> is founded what I have often before drawn attention
> to: the negativity of well-being and happiness, in
> antithesis to the positivity of pain.
> I therefore know of no greater absurdity than
> that absurdity which characterizes almost all meta-
> physical systems: that of explaining evil as some-
> thing negative. For evil is precisely that which is
> positive, that which makes itself palpable; and good,
> on the other hand, i. e., all happiness and gratifi-
> cation, is that which is negative, the mere abolition
> of a desire and extinction of a pain. [71]

This excerpt bespeaks an outlook that was blind, evidently, to many of life's little pleasures. But Schopenhauer's view-point is validated by a host of respectable intellects, includ-ing many of the philosophers and religious thinkers who have been discussed earlier. Too, his main point should not be obscured. Schopenhauer is not saying "there is no such thing as happiness" so much as he is saying that there can be un-happiness in advancement, joy in retreat. It hurts to walk into a wall and have evil make itself "palpable." On the other hand, it feels good to fall asleep at the end of a long day and experience "the extinction of a pain."

The following chapters abound with literary examples of this fundamental monistic premise, but it would be appro-priate to give one here as well. I am thinking of The Scarlet

Letter, in which the evils are palpable: the lovers' sin,
Hester's punishment, Chillingworth's revenge.  On the other
hand, the good occurrences in the novel all take the form of
retreats from the world: Dimmesdale's joyful death, Hester's
nunlike repose, Pearl's departure for England.

Schopenhauer himself was a splendid if hyperbolic
critic of literature.  Here is McGill's paraphrase of Schopenhauer's basic criteria:

> Thus the world proves itself a regular waxworks of
> horrors, a raree-show of agonized human beings
> smiling through their wretchedness out of pride or
> shame or for the sake of appearances.  Should any-
> one doubt this sad portrayal, a consideration of art,
> "that true mirror of life and the world," will soon
> convince him.  In novels, poetry, and tragic drama
> in particular, he will find proof enough.  Thus
> every novelist worries his hero with all the vexa-
> tions and sufferings he can conceive and continues
> his miseries to the last chapter.  Why?  In order
> that he shall stand out as real and convincing.
> Would it not be far more entertaining if the hero
> were allowed to live a life of pleasure with an early
> gratification of his desires?  No, for pleasure is
> shallow, illusory, the mere absence of pain.  Novels
> laid in a happy garden of Epicurus, and there have
> been some, are consequently hollow and incredible,
> and horribly wearisome.  Tragedies and poetry are
> under the same sad compulsion.  Suffering is the
> theme and it is this which holds us.  Only in lighter,
> shorter pieces can the sense of pleasure be sustained
> and even here it is difficult.  Dante in the Paradiso,
> taking refuge in mystical and therefore unintelligible
> pleasures, managed, in a manner, to keep it up,
> but its force was far less than that of the Inferno. [72]

Since it is the fervent if unspoken hope of most of us
that life will prove to be something more than "a regular wax-
works of horrors," we must look at the cultural context of
Schopenhauer's remarks if we are to understand their successful reception.  Of primary importance is a sense of what
it was that Schopenhauer opposed.  Schopenhauer's philosophy
was a direct affront, not to the mild and balanced outlook of
ordinary times, but to the overweening optimism and energy
of the Renaissance and the Enlightenment.  The sanguinary
thinkers who propounded such ideas served a positive purpose,

to be sure. But how dismaying their outlook must have been to the poor, the sick, the downcast. And even among the comfortable and the well-off there were those who knew that Enlightenment thought was, if admirable, limited nonetheless. To be rational and purposeful is good, but there are other qualities in human nature, just as there are unforeseen difficulties in daily living that rationalism and purposefulness alone cannot overcome. The writings of Schopenhauer, far from being discouraging, thus offer aid and comfort to those in whose faces the finger of Enlightenment philosophy has been wagged too long. R. J. Hollingdale says that "many found it a great relief to cast off for once the obbligato optimism of our culture and to face the possibility that things may not be all for the best."[73] In this way, Schopenhauer's philosophy previews the teachings of Freud. It is surprising and, in a way, amusing to learn what Freud promised the successful analysand. The goal of psychoanalysis, in Freud's own words, is "transforming your hysterical misery into common unhappiness."[74] Not ecstasy, not release, but the "common unhappiness" of the average citizen plagued by bills and backaches.

My own understanding of Freud is that he is concerned not, as is popularly assumed, with sex but with the workings of the libido. Even that word means "sex drive" to most people, but only because the popularizers who have pretended that Freud is interested in sex and nothing else have perverted the meaning that Freud intended. In his little essay "On Transience," Freud defines libido simply as our "capacity for love."[75] And it is in this essay that Freud probably discusses most lucidly--that is, in nontechnical, nonpsychoanalytic terms--his findings on the confused nature of our desires. The essay begins:

> Not long ago I went on a summer walk through a smiling countryside in the company of a taciturn friend and of a young but already famous poet [a footnote identifies the time and place as August 1913, in the Dolomites, but fails to name Freud's companions]. The poet admired the beauty of the scene around us but felt no joy in it. He was disturbed by the thought that all this beauty was fated to extinction, that it would vanish when winter came, like all human beauty and all the beauty and splendor that men have created or may create. All that he would otherwise have loved and admired seemed to him to be shorn of its worth by the transience which was its doom.[76]

But Freud disputes the poet's view that a realization of
the transient nature of beauty results in a loss of its
worth.

> On the contrary, an increase... ! Limitation in the
> possibility of an enjoyment raises the value of the
> enjoyment. ... The beauty of the human form and
> face vanish for ever in the course of our own lives,
> but their evanescence only lends them a fresh
> charm. [77]

Sounding more like a Zen master than a psychoanalyst, Freud
asks rhetorically if the things we have lost in our lives have
"really ceased to have any worth for us because they have
proved so perishable and so unresistant?" Freud's own feelings on the matter are clear:

> To many of us this seems to be so, but ... wrongly,
> in my view. I believe that those who think thus,
> and seem ready to make a permanent renunciation
> because what was precious has proved not to be
> lasting, are simply in a state of mourning for what
> is lost. Mourning, as we know, however painful
> it may be, comes to a spontaneous end. When it
> has renounced everything that has been lost, then
> it has consumed itself, and our libido is once more
> free (in so far as we are still young and active) to
> replace the lost objects by fresh ones equally or
> still more precious. [78]

It is interesting to consider just what is being advised
here. Written as it was in November 1915, at the height of
Freud's intellectual and professional maturity, "On Transience" counsels detachment rather than knowledge. Only three
pages in length, this essay admits the fundamental wronghead-
edness of our nature ("to many of us this seems to be so"),
but instead of telling us to locate our true objects of desire,
it simply says that we should treat all objects equally--that
is, appreciatively yet with detachment.

There can be no doubt as to why this is the least successful of Freud's teachings. Our culture emphasizes achievement, perfection. It emphasizes answers. If we are unhappy,
surely we can find out why. The cure is obtainable even if
it is expensive--indeed, the more expensive the cure, the
better it will be. The recent boom in the counseling industry,

with the proliferation of advice (for a price) through books,
articles, agencies, and television programs, is proof simple
of the basic law of commerce: that which can be marketed
will be. At bottom, these psychologists are no different from
any other business people. Their job is to make us want
their product, to believe that our lives will be incomplete
if we do not buy what they sell.

In a book aptly titled What Went Wrong? Why Hasn't
Having More Made People Happier?, Jeremy Seabrook offers
a painfully truthful analysis of present-day marketing techniques, ones that can be used to peddle anything from counseling to stereos. His book deals with life in Great Britain, but
this passage on newspaper advertisements applies equally to
life in this country.

> Things are more than better; they are perfect.
> A colour supplement opened at random in December
> 1977 offered this flow of superlatives--best loved,
> most desired, handsome, desirable, excellent, lov-
> ing care, original, fun, stimulating, exciting, best,
> sophisticated, creative, convenient, fascinating,
> classic, impeccable, new, fresh, high quality, sat-
> isfying, magnificent, masterpiece, unique, joy, style,
> trust, happy, finest, most distinguished ever, best,
> perfect, enjoyable, quality, most distinctive, bril-
> liant, most beautiful in the world, a better start in
> life, super, sheer pleasure, genius, real, natural,
> invaluable, countless new possibilities, well-being,
> goodness. It doesn't matter what any of these
> words refers to; what does matter is that they all
> describe inanimate objects, and many of them are
> borrowed from the kind of experiences that have
> traditionally been felt to belong to humanity, not to
> the realm of its artefacts. The transference of
> human attributes to things, their power to bestow
> satisfactions which previously only people were
> thought capable of giving, is a visible part of the
> process of dehumanizing others, and substituting
> commodities for the debased humanity. It is not
> the things themselves that are at fault: it is only
> when the terms on which they are available adversely
> affects people. [79]

One cringes as Seabrook's list of superlatives is read. Singly,
they attract even the most sophisticated (who does not want
the "best"?). Cumulatively, they cut like blows from a whip,

since they remind us not only of the ugliness of our culture
but also of our own complicity in it. Taken out of context
by Seabrook, these superlatives remind us of the not-so-secret
goal of the merchandisers: to cause us to think that what
they have will satisfy our desires at last.

Opposed to this feverish desiring is the passive method
of Freud. His biographer tells us that Freud experimented
with many of the therapeutic techniques of his day but found
them all too meddlesome. He tried but quickly abandoned
electrical stimulation, and hypnosis he termed "a coarsely
interfering method." Instead, says Jones, Freud chose
simply "to look and listen," confident that "it was the passive
method that succeeded, not the active one."[80] In a 1912 essay, "Recommendations to Physicians Practicing Psychoanalysis," Freud describes what one writer has called "the aim-
less, Zen-like state of desirelessness" that the analyst must
cultivate.[81] "It consists simply in not directing one's notice
to anything in particular and in maintaining the same 'evenly
suspended attention' (as I have called it) in the face of all
that one hears," writes Freud. He cautions the analyst not
to let anything, especially his own ambition, get in the way
of the movement of "his own unconscious like a receptive
organ toward the transmitting unconscious of the patient."[82]
In analysis, as in any of the esoteric philosophies and religions discussed earlier, illumination is attained only through
disciplined awareness.

★

I began this chapter with Freud's pronouncement that "America
is a mistake" and then qualified the statement by pointing out
that to Freud everything was a mistake, or at least everything
was mistaken, since everything has a surface meaning as well
as a deeper one that is more difficult to apprehend. To
Freud, America was simply more of a mistake than other
countries were. And just as this realization may have been
more apparent to a Jew than to a Christian, as I also argued,
so it seems more likely to have been made by a European
than an American. American pessimism is vital but isolated;
indeed, the vitality of a book like Moby-Dick is directly at-
tributable to the anger felt by the isolated genius who wrote
it. On the other hand, there is a European tradition of pessimism that runs from the classics forward to Freud's day
and beyond. Matthew Arnold tells us in "Dover Beach" that
he hears the same "eternal note of sadness" that brought to
the mind of Sophocles "the turbid ebb and flow / of human

misery," and Thomas Hardy was fond of quoting Sophocles'
dictum, "Not to have been born is best." This pessimistic
strain found in poets and playwrights was reinforced in the
ordinary citizen by the virtually endless series of wars that
one associates with the European continent. For our purpose
the greatest of these was World War I. In essence, modern
culture in the West found itself back where it began, in the
plague years of the fourteenth century, helpless, leaderless,
bereft. Freud wrote "On Transience" in order to console
those who were devastated by the conflict, and his description
of the loss makes apparent the intensity of the deprivation
felt by an entire culture.

> My conversation with the poet took place in the
> summer before the war. A year later the war
> broke out and robbed the world of its beauties. It
> destroyed not only the beauty of the countrysides
> through which it passed and the works of art which
> it met with on its path but it also shattered our
> pride in the achievements of our civilization, our
> admiration for many philosophers and artists and
> our hopes of a final triumph over the differences
> between nations and races. It tarnished the lofty
> impartiality of our science, it revealed our instincts
> in all their nakedness and let loose the evil spirits
> within us which we thought had been tamed for ever
> by centuries of continuous education by the noblest
> minds. It made our country small again and made
> the rest of the world far remote. It robbed us of
> very much that we had loved, and showed us how
> ephemeral were many things that we had regarded
> as changeless. [83]

There had been other wars, of course. But Paul Fussell reminds us that "the Great War was more ironic than any
before or since. It was a hideous embarrassment to the pre-
vailing Meliorist myth which had dominated the public consciousness for a century. It reversed the idea of Progress."[84]
With little exaggeration, Fussell might have added the phrase
"though not in America" to his last sentence. Writers both
domestic and foreign have commented on the comparative
clarity and seamlessness of the American face, an innocence
of visage in a country largely unmarked by war, which is to
say by history. Removed as we are, we still believe in progress. In Without Marx or Jesus, Jean-François Revel observes that in America individuals believe they can better
their circumstances, whereas in a typical European society

the average person feels trapped, that the best one can do is to slip around one obstacle or another from time to time. [85] In Europe, one feels that others are in charge, whereas in America, one feels that one is in charge of oneself.

Yet how terrible it is to be in charge all the time! Tocqueville observed that Americans are always on duty, that they are always "serious and almost sad."

> In aristocratic communities the people readily give themselves up to bursts of tumultuous and boister-ous gaiety, which shake off at once the recollection of their privations. The inhabitants of democracies are not fond of being thus violently broken in upon, and they never lose sight of themselves without re-gret. Instead of these frivolous delights they pre-fer those more serious and silent amusements which are like business and which do not drive business wholly out of their minds. An American, instead of going in a leisure hour to dance merrily at some place of public resort, as the fellows of his class continue to do throughout the greater part of Europe, shuts himself up at home to drink. He thus enjoys two pleasures; he can go on thinking of his business and can get drunk decently by his own fireside.

This goal-oriented, purposeful aspect of the American character is nicely illustrated in an incident in Two Years Before the Mast, in which Richard Henry Dana contrasts an Italian ship to the American one on which he served. The Italian ship was much smaller than the American vessel, yet there were three times as many crew. The American ship was run more efficiently, yet the crew was silent and seemed discontent. The Italians divided the work among more sailors than did the Americans and they were doing something else differently as well, notes Dana. They were singing.

# 2

## "BARTLEBY THE SCRIVENER"

---

"I would prefer not to."

It is appropriate to begin our examination of specific texts
with Melville's "Bartleby the Scrivener: A Story of Wall
Street" (1853). In its way, "Bartleby" is as American as
The Adventures of Huckleberry Finn. Melville's un-storylike
story is a statement on work, and work, as the observations
by Tocqueville and Dana at the end of the previous chapter
suggest, is one of America's raisons d'être.

Work is also the white space on the map of literature.
Writers write about what they know: writers drink a good
deal, for instance, so there is a lot of drinking in books.
But writers do not work, or at least most of them do not
have eight-to-five, baloney-on-white-bread, Jones-you're-late-
again jobs. Neither do most readers of serious literature,
meaning college professors and their students. They may
have much to do, but at least the average professor or student does not have to check with the foreman before going out
to get a cup of coffee or a haircut. So, if writers don't
work, and readers don't work, who is to notice that work is
the single essential element of human existence that is almost
totally neglected in literature, or care?

The treatment or neglect of work in literature is almost a moot point before the Industrial Revolution. But thereafter, even when work is mentioned in literature, it appears
often as a sort of novelty. In "Pied Beauty," for example,
Gerard Manley Hopkins praises God for "all things counter,
original, spare, strange," including "all trades, their gear
and tackle and trim."[1] The point is clear: the worker's
equipment, as opposed to, say, the pen and paper of the poet,
amazes in its variety. But no doubt the exhausted worker
looks at tools with an eye somewhat more jaundiced than that
of the delighted poet.

52

Further, when the tediousness of work--the unrelent-
ing boredom of it yet the unflagging necessity for it--is represented in literature (as it rarely is), the representation is
usually not only indirect but also handled in such a way that
its main purpose is to suggest the contrast between work and
something pleasant, namely, leisure and freedom.  In Henry
James's The Princess Casamassima, when Captain Sholto,
who has retired from the service and is free to hobnob with
aristocrats, asks the bookbinder Hyacinth Robinson if he in-
tends to spend the winter in London, Hyacinth stares at him
in wonder until Sholto catches his mistake and mumbles,  "'Oh,
of course you've got your work, and that sort of thing.'"[2]
Later, when Hyacinth visits the Princess at Medley, her
country estate, he finds it necessary to insist that he be allowed to return to his job, for the Princess cannot understand why he doesn't want to stay on indefinitely:

> "Princess," he then said, "you've no idea--how
> should you have?--into the midst of what abject,
> pitiful preoccupations you thrust yourself.  I've
> no clothes."
> "What do you want of money?  This isn't an
> hotel."
> "Every day I stay here I lose a day's wages.
> I live on my wages from day to day."
> "Let me then give you your wages.  You'll work
> for me."
> "What do you mean--work for you?"
> "You'll bind all my books."[3]

Hyacinth does what many men in his circumstances would do
--that is, he quits his job and stays on to enjoy the pleasures
of Medley and the Princess, much to the annoyance of the
practical old doyenne Madame Grandoni, who sees correctly
that Hyacinth's irresponsible step is the first in a series
that will lead to his ultimate downfall.

The Princess Casamassima is James's farthest pene-
tration into the territory of the Naturalists, a school of writers whose sympathies are said to lie with the working class.
But because of their need to deal with humanity at its most
debased, the Naturalists are more interested in the formerly
employed or the unemployable than in any other group.  Insofar as Naturalism deals with work at all, it depicts a vast
social, political, and economic system of which workers are
a necessary but replaceable part.  Frank Norris's "A Deal
in Wheat," for example, is ostensibly the story of Sam

Lewiston, a ruined farmer who seeks and gains employment
in Chicago but is thrown out of work by hard times. Yet
the story focuses not on Lewiston's misery but on the specu-
lations of Hornung and Truslow, the plutocrats who manipulate
the price of grain for their own profit and everyone else's
loss. Lewiston gains an insight into the system and sees
that he has been caught "in the cogs and wheels of a great
and terrible engine," which is one of the Naturalists' favorite
metaphors.[4] But he is happy to get a job again, this time
with the street-cleaning brigade. Hornung and Truslow go on
as they have before, "jovial, contented, enthroned, and unas-
sailable."[5] But Lewiston disappears into the anonymity of
his class.

For the worker, nothing changes: the wheels grind
on. When Jurgis Rudkus of Upton Sinclair's The Jungle is
hired by a meat packer, he thinks to himself: "Had he not
just gotten a job, and become a sharer in all this activity,
a cog in this marvellous machine?"[6] But of course the machine spits him out when his usefulness is ended. Jurgis
and his family are shown to be totally helpless, totally controlled by external forces, because in a novel of social injustice the poor and unskilled must not be able to help themselves, or else where is the injustice? Everything that happens to Jurgis, good as well as bad, is determined by forces
external to him. He gets and loses jobs, he becomes a
strong-arm man and a thief, he goes from crime to politics
(between which there is little distinction, according to Sinclair), each time rising above his sorrows and then sinking
down into them even more deeply than before because of the
injustice done to him by one boss or another. In the end,
he is spellbound by a Socialist orator and joins the party.
But it is important to recognize that he is acted on by the
orator as he is by everyone else: he becomes dopey and
glassy-eyed before the orator's promises as he once did at
the thought of a new house and fine clothes. Yes, Jurgis
will be a Socialist. But what choice does he have? Social-
ism seems less like the right thing and more like the only
thing that remains. Like Lewiston, Jurgis is part of what
H. L. Mencken called "a vast mass of undifferentiated human
blanks, bossed by demagogues."[7] For all their vaunted sym-
pathy with the lower class, the Naturalists seem more interested in villifying the system than in creating working-class
heroes.

A contemporary Naturalistic novel, Charles Bukowski's
semiautobiographical Post Office, portrays with humor and

insight one worker's futile struggle with the system.   But as
usual there is no change, no difference:   the novel begins
with the words "it began as a mistake" (referring to the narrator's job with the post office) and ends:   "Maybe I'll write
a novel, I thought.   And then I did."[8]   The suggestion that
the narrator will repeat his experiences, even on paper, has
a bad-dream quality, which is reinforced by the narrative itself.   For like Lewiston and Jurgis, Bukowski's narrator is
alternately in and out of work, trying to escape the institu-
tionalized madness of the system yet finding himself caught
up in it again and again.

When a well-made piece of literature not only discusses the unpleasant realities described above but also offers
a healthy intellectual and emotional response to them, one realizes how few works of this sort there are.   Such a work is
Hayden Carruth's poem "Emergency Haying."   For all the
pleasure that Gerard Manley Hopkins took in the contemplation of workers and their trades, he might have written a
poem like this one had he ever put in the kind of day Hayden
Carruth describes.

> Coming home with the last load I ride standing
> on the wagon tongue, behind the tractor
> in hot exhaust, lank with sweat,
>
> my arms strung
> awkwardly along the hayrack, cruciform.
> Almost 500 bales we've put up
>
> this afternoon, Marshall and I.
> And of course I think of another who hung
> like this on another cross.   My hands are torn
>
> by baling twine, not nails, and my side is pierced
> by my ulcer, not a lance.   The acid in my throat
> is only hayseed.   Yet exhaustion and the way
>
> my body hangs from twisted shoulders, suspended
> on two points of pain in the rising
> monoxide, recall that greater suffering. [9]

Carruth's persona thinks of "those who have done slave labor"
and recalls a friend whose grandmother cut cane with a ma-
chete until the day she cut off her own hand and threw it at
the sky.   Concluding, he asks:

> ... And who
> is the Christ now, who
>
> if not I? It must be so. My strength
> is legion. And I stand up high
> on the wagon tongue in my whole bones to say
>
> woe to you, watch out
> you sons of bitches who would drive men and women
> to the fields where they can only die. [10]

The contrast I have drawn between Hopkins and Carruth should
be balanced by a comparison as well, for "Emergency Haying," its disgust with work notwithstanding, is a poem at least
as religious as any Hopkins ever wrote. Only Carruth's
Christ is the political activist, the one who brings not peace
but a sword.

For all his insight, however, for all his fire and
feistiness, Carruth's persona does nothing more than make
a statement about work. Everybody talks about work, but
nobody does anything about it. The world's books are full
of quiet, dependable clerks, such as Akaky Akakievich of
Gogol's "The Overcoat," of whom the reader is told:

> It would be hard to find a man who so lived for
> his job. It would not be enough to say that he
> worked conscientiously--he worked with love. There,
> in his copying, he found an interesting, pleasant
> world for himself and his delight was reflected in
> his face. He had his favorites among the letters
> of the alphabet and, when he came to them, he
> would chuckle, wink and help them along with his
> lips as they were formed by his pen. [11]

The ill luck that befalls Akaky is due to the loss of his overcoat and the bureaucracy's inability to help him recover it.
His fellow workers and his supervisor are prankish and in-
sensitive, much in the manner of their counterparts in "Bartleby," but their high jinks mean nothing to Akaky, who would
have been happy to go on indefinitely, copying his favorite
letters.

Even Gregor Samsa, of Kafka's "The Metamorphosis,"
realizes that his work, loathsome as it is to him, is nonetheless necessary to his existence. On the day that he wakes
and finds himself transformed into a gigantic insect, his first
thoughts are of his job.

> Oh, God, he thought, what an exhausting job
> I've picked on [sic]! Traveling about day in, day
> out. It's much more irritating work than doing the
> actual business in the office, and on top of that
> there's the trouble of constant traveling, of worry-
> ing about train connections, the bed and irregular
> meals, casual acquaintances that are always new
> and never become intimate friends. The devil take
> it all![12]

But when his supervisor arrives to upbraid him, Gregor's
reaction is that of the ordinary wage earner: "Gregor perceived that the chief clerk must on no account be allowed to
go away in this frame of mind if his position in the firm
were not to be endangered to the utmost."[13] His work is
certainly a major part of a world so absurd that Gregor has
become an insect in response to it, but Gregor does not pause
to reflect on such matters. Insect or no, he wants to punch
in on time.

In contrast, there is Bartleby. Pleasing his employer
seems to be the least of Bartleby's concerns, although it is
some time before the reader discovers this. Before Bartleby
is even introduced to the story, Melville takes pains to describe Bartleby's employer, the setting in which he will work,
and his co-workers. He even alludes to the larger world of
business in order to make it clear that "Bartleby the Scrivener," in addition to being a human drama like any other
fiction, is a treatise on work as well.

The likably self-centered employer/narrator finds his
own job pleasant and easy:

> I am a man who, from his youth upwards, has been
> filled with a profound conviction that the easiest way
> of life is the best. Hence, though I belong to a
> profession proverbially energetic and nervous, even
> to turbulence, at times, yet nothing of that sort
> have I ever suffered to invade my peace. I am
> one of those unambitious lawyers who never ad-
> dresses a jury, or in any way draws down public
> applause; but, in the cool tranquillity of a snug re-
> treat, do a snug business among rich men's bonds,
> and mortgages, and title-deeds. All who know me,
> consider me an eminently <u>safe</u> man.[14]

Bartleby's boss is a political appointee, a Master of Chancery,

one who settles estates and the like.   Concerning his appoint-
ment, he says, "it was not a very arduous office, but very
pleasantly remunerative."15   And so it is usually for the employer.

But the work of the three employees--Turkey, Nippers, and Ginger Nut--is boring and frustrating.   Not sur-
prisingly, each of these has developed one or more idiosyncrasies, which, though caused by the tedium of work, allow
him in some small way to relieve it.   Turkey is a secret
boozer who throws himself into a frenzy of work after he has
drunk his lunch.   He makes a racket with his chair, spills
the sand he uses as a blotter, splits his pens and throws
them on the floor, splashes ink on the documents in his
charge.   Nippers grinds his teeth audibly and adjusts his
desk compulsively.   He does not drink, like Turkey, but the
narrator observes that, "for Nippers, brandy-and-water were
altogether superfluous."16   Ginger Nut has assorted duties
and a desk of his own, "but he did not use it much,"17 for
he, Turkey, and Nippers cooperate in a work-relieving conspiracy.   The latter two send Ginger Nut to fetch apples and
cookies all day long, which is to say that these little errands
are to him what drinking, teeth-grinding, and fidgeting are to
the other two.   These idiosyncrasies are work-induced ways
to make work something other than what it is, namely, a
repetitive, reductive, personality-destroying yet absolutely
necessary (and all the more hateful because it is necessary)
bore.   It is little wonder that the terms used to describe
these workers' habits are pathological in nature.   Their twitch-
ing and rushing about is described as "fits," "paroxysms,"
and "flurried rashnesses."17

The arrival of Bartleby amidst all this noise and fury
is like the entrance of a monk into a madhouse.   He is "neat,"
"respectable," and "sedate."18   Best of all, he is a sedulous
worker.   "At first, Bartleby did an extraordinary quantity of
writing."19   But there is something unhealthy about his application:   "As if long famishing for something to copy, he
seemed to gorge himself on my documents [says the narra-
tor].   There was no pause for digestion....   He wrote on
silently, palely, mechanically."20   Bartleby, who has had at
least one other job that we know of, continues this way for
three days before his protests begin.   It is as though he has
taken this job in a last attempt to convince himself that work
is worthwhile and has thrown himself into his labors with a
determined frenzy that expires upon his realizing, once again,
that boredom and frustration are inevitable if unpleasant con-
juncts of earning one's daily bread.

Much has been written about Bartleby's meek protest --the phrase "I would prefer not to," with which he responds to every request or command--and many critical articles attempt to link Bartleby's protest with such maladies as autism, schizophrenia, hebephrenia, and agoraphobia as well as with other, more vaguely defined causes, such as Melville's own "suicidal" tendencies. It is not difficult, of course, to see Bartleby's seeming negativism as part of a larger syndrome of ill health. But all manifestations of personality have two names, one approving and one disapproving. What is withdrawal to one observer may be self-possession to another, and so on. Bartleby's naysaying, along with his self-containment and his refusal to leave the office, may conform to a pathological syndrome, but it can also be viewed positively. More than that, Bartleby's behavior can be seen and is most fruitfully and rewardingly seen as active, efficacious, and life-enhancing rather passive, futile, and life-denying.

Not all of the "Bartleby" criticism is negative, of course (though certainly the best-known studies are). A number of essays establish correlations between Bartleby's behavior and some of the varieties of religious and philosophic practice described in Chapter 1 of this study. An essay by Saburo Yamaya, for example, attributes the stone imagery in "Bartleby" to a discussion of Buddhist quietism in Pierre Bayle's Dictionnaire Historique et Critique, an English translation of which Melville had bought in 1849. Yamaya cites the following passage from Bayle:

> The great lords and the most illustrious persons
> suffered themselves to be so infatuated with this
> [Buddhist] Quietism, that they believed insensibility
> to be the way to perfection and beatitude and that
> the nearer a man came to the nature of a block or
> a stone, the greater progress he made, the more
> he was like the first principle, into which he was
> to return. 21

A second writer, H. Bruce Franklin, believes that the Oriental ascetic Bartleby is modeled on is the Saniassi, a Hindu rather than a Buddhist, and that Thomas Maurice's Indian Antiquities is the source. According to Franklin,

> Maurice describes in detail the systematic with-
> drawal from the world practiced by the Saniassi,
> and many details have a surprising--and grotesquely
> humorous--correspondence to the systematic with-

drawal from the world practiced by Bartleby. For
instance, in the fifth stage the Saniassi "eats only
one particular kind of food during the day and night,
but as often as he pleases." Bartleby "lives, then,
on ginger-nuts ... never eats a dinner, properly
speaking; he must be a vegetarian, then, but no; he
never eats even vegetables, he eats nothing but
ginger-nuts." "During the last three days," the
Saniassi "neither eats nor drinks." During Bartleby's last few days, he prefers not to eat. [22]

But these correspondences between Bartleby's withdrawal and
that of the Saniassi are less important than their shared outlook.

[Maurice] observes that one of the principal ways
in which the Saniassi is distinguished from the Yogi
is "by the calm, the silent, dignity with which he
suffers the series of complicated evils through
which he is ordained to toil." The Saniassi "can
only be fed by the charity of others"; "he must
himself make no exertion, nor feel any solicitude
for existence upon this contaminated orb." The
Saniassis' design "is to detach their thoughts from
all concern about sublunary objects; to be indifferent
to hunger and thirst; to be insensible to shame and
reproach."[23]

These words could just as well be applied to Bartleby as to
Maurice's Hindu ascetic. As his life unwinds, Bartleby answers every remonstrance with calm and dignity. He lets
others have their will with him; like the Saniassi, he will
save them, if he can, by refusing to save himself. Franklin
continues:

Perhaps most important to the judgment of Bartleby is the Saniassis' "incessant efforts ... to stifle
every ebullition of human passion, and live upon
earth as if they were already, and in reality, disembodied." This may at once help account for
Bartleby's appearing as a "ghost" or as "cadaver-
ous" to the narrator and explain what ethical time
he follows, for "it is the boast of the Saniassi to
sacrifice every human feeling and passion at the
shrine of devotion." Like Bartleby, the Saniassi
"is no more to be soothed by the suggestions of
adulation in its most pleasing form, than he is to

> be terrified by the loudest clamours of reproach....
> By long habits of indifference, he becomes inani-
> mate as a piece of wood or stone" [thus this image,
> so important to "Bartleby," appears in Indian An-
> tiquities as well as in Bayle's Dictionnaire]. 24

And yet these references to Buddhists and Hindus stick
in the craws of many readers, just as the discussions of various phobias are distasteful to others. Torn between the possibility that Bartleby is either an Oriental saint or a home-
grown madman, it is little wonder that the hapless reader
gives up in despair, preferring to let Melville's puzzling
character be anyone, everyone, no one--as Bartleby himself seems to prefer--at all.

A recent book is entitled Bartleby the Inscrutable: A
Collection of Commentary on Herman Melville's "Bartleby the
Scrivener." It is a book that belongs in every academic library, for it deals comprehensively with a work that is central to our culture. It contains contemporary reviews of
"Bartleby," critical essays, and an invaluable annotated check-
list of some two hundred sixty-two interpretations of Melville's
puzzling tale. Yet one cannot help but enter a demurrer, not
so much against Bartleby the Inscrutable itself as against a
type of thinking it may promote. At a time when the pres-
ences of Joyce, Pound, and Eliot are still felt, we are only
doing what we must when we encourage the widest possible
range of response to works of literature. But we go too far
if we seem to say that any intellectually honest interpretation
is as good as the next, which is exactly what this collection
seems to say. "By no means is this book meant to conclude
anything about the story, aside from its inscrutability," says
the introduction to Bartleby the Inscrutable. 25 If we agree
with this, then we are given to think that the inscrutable and
the sublime are practically the same. It makes more sense
to say that between a single restrictive interpretation of any
work and an infinity of interpretations lies a finite number of
workable interpretations, the best of which is not only the
one that brings out the full potential of the text rather than
restricting or narrowing it but also the one that coexists with
the greatest number of other, equally valid interpretations.

Probably no other work in Western literature tests
this idea as well as "Bartleby," for surely no other work has
attracted a greater number of bizarre readings, the greater
part of which makes Bartleby out to be a sick man, a loser,
an apostle of negation and despair. Yet how different, how

how much more rewarding is Bartleby's story if it is approached from another angle. From a positive rather than a negative viewpoint, Bartleby is protesting the boring, frustrating, exploitative job he has, and he is doing so in accordance with one of the most time-honored and effective ways of protest: civil disobedience. "Bartleby the Scrivener" was published in 1856, seven years after Thoreau's famous essay (originally called "On Resistance to Civil Government"). Without suggesting that Melville had Thoreau's treatise in mind, we must assume that Melville would have known not only about the essay itself but also about its political and philosophical background, given the common intellectual interests and reading habits of the Transcendentalists and those who swam in their wake.[26] And indeed, "Bartleby the Scrivener" reads like a textbook illustration of civil disobedience. It may even be said that Bartleby's protest has greater effect than Thoreau's failure to pay his poll tax, since Thoreau's jailers go largely unmoved by his protest, whereas Bartleby's self-sacrifice causes his employer to see things differently and develop compassion.

The first requirement of civil disobedience is gentleness. Bartleby's choice of language, as the following excerpt illustrates, is particularly important in this respect.

> "Bartleby," [said the employer], "Ginger Nut is away; just step around to the Post Office, won't you? (it was but a three minutes' walk), and see if there is anything for me."
> "I would prefer not to."
> "You will not?"
> "I prefer not."[27]

The second requirement is persistence, of which there can be no doubt. Bartleby not only refuses to obey orders, he also refuses to leave the office. Taken to prison, he refuses favors, he refuses food, he refuses to speak--ultimately, he refuses to live.

Which leads to the third requirement, self-sacrifice. A sharp distinction must be drawn between political disrupters who seek amnesty as part of their platform for change and such practitioners of classic civil disobedience as Gandhi and Martin Luther King, who were willing to be jailed and even die for their beliefs.

Of course, the practice of these virtues is to no avail

if they have no effect on the person or institution toward
whom the civil disobedience is directed.   Yet Bartleby's
protest is effective.   In the early days of Bartleby's refusal
to work, the employer notes that "with any other man I should
have flown outright into a dreadful passion, scorned all further
words, and thrust him ignominiously from my presence.   But
there was something about Bartleby that not only strangely
disarmed me, but, in a wonderful manner, touched and dis-
concerted me."[28]   Gradually, Bartleby succeeds in "training"
the employer:

> Now and then, in the eagerness of dispatching press-
> ing business, I would inadvertently summon Bartleby,
> in a short, rapid tone, to put his finger, say, on
> the incipient tie of a bit of red tape with which I
> was about compressing some papers.   Of course,
> from behind the screen the usual answer, "I pre-
> fer not to," was sure to come; and then, how could
> a human creature, with the common infirmities of
> our nature, refrain from bitterly exclaiming upon
> such perverseness--such unreasonableness.   How-
> ever, every added repulse of this sort which I re-
> ceived only tended to lessen the probability of my
> repeating the inadvertence. [29]

The words "inadvertently" and "inadvertent" are emphasized
by me to bring out the employer's sense of his own inatten-
tion and carelessness, qualities that are replaced by mindfulness and awareness once the teachings of Bartleby begin to
hit home.   As the story approaches its end, the employer
realizes that Bartleby is more powerful than he is:

> The idea came upon me of his possibly turning out
> a long-lived man, and keep occupying my chambers,
> and denying my authority; and perplexing my vis-
> itors; and scandalizing my professional reputation;
> and casting a general gloom over the premises;
> keeping body and soul together to the last upon his
> savings (for doubtless he spent but half a dime a
> day), and in the end perhaps outlive me, and claim
> possession of my office by right of his perpetual
> occupancy. [30]

Transformed, the once-uncaring employer offers to assist
Bartleby in finding some other line of work, but the unco-
operative clerk has made his commitment and refuses once
more.   So strong is the force of Bartleby's character that

when the employer goes to visit him in prison and, on finding him dead, touches him, he is shocked as though by an
electrical charge: "I felt his hand, when a tingling shiver
ran up my arm and down my spine to my feet."[31]

It must be said here that undoubtedly I, too, would
have gone on indefinitely in the belief that "Bartleby" was
about anything other than work had I not once found myself
in a setting similar to that of Melville's story. This was
at a point in my life when I abandoned temporarily the lei-
surely routine of the English professor (which included, in
my case, numerous less-than-successful attempts to understand and teach "Bartleby") for an office job. Suddenly, it
all came clear. Eight-to-five work in a crowded, window-
less office, where the threat of censure is as pervasive as
the glare of fluorescence, is inimical to the human spirit.
Those who maintained their equanimity under such conditions
were few in number, and they amazed me. Most of the
others had coping mechanisms analogous to those of Turkey,
Nippers, and Ginger Nut. One woman cleared her throat
constantly; it was a kind of glottal fidget that drove those
around her crazy. Another worker would shout "Errands!"
at least once a day and then fire through the door like a
cannonball; he always returned, but never with any evidence
of having satisfied these imaginary calls to duty. Valium
and other tranquilizers steadied many a hand; alcohol caused
others to tremble.

To me, the job explained "Bartleby," just as "Bartleby" explained the job.[32] What had happened in the lives of
both the real and the fictional workers was that a world of
blind achievement had come between them and their own tranquility. "What can we gain by sailing to the moon if we are
not able to cross the abyss that separates us from ourselves?"
asked Thomas Merton in Chapter 1 of this study, writing of
the Desert Fathers. Melville himself, in a darker mood,
opines that "in the soul of man there lies one insular Tahiti,
full of peace and joy, but encompassed by all the horrors of
the half known life. God keep thee! Push not off from that
isle, thou canst never return!" These lines from Moby-Dick
are but a more forceful paraphrase of Marcus Aurelius' Stoic
admonition, also discussed in the previous chapter, to "remember to retire into this little territory of thine own." That
is all that Bartleby does.

## THE MILL ON THE FLOSS

---

"And so it came to pass that she often lost the spirit
of humility by being excessive in the outward act. "

All that is missing from my monistic reading of "Bartleby"
is an indication in the story of his actual conversion, a precise fixing of the moment when Bartleby decided to forswear
conventional working-class goals and begin a life of asceticism and protest.  How helpful it would be if some scholar
unearthed the real "Bartleby" manuscript, the one in which
our narrator finds a diary, say, where Bartleby has recorded
his intent to emulate the Saniassis, the Buddhist Quietists,
Thoreau himself.  Such an announcement would clear up the
mystery forever.  So Melville, in his cunning, made none.

The next work to be considered, George Eliot's The
Mill on the Floss, differs from "Bartleby" in innumerable
ways, not the least of which is in its inclusion of a lengthy,
detailed, and heartfelt account of the heroine's conversion to
a monistic outlook.  Such an account would be out of place
in Melville, of course, who accepted most creeds and was
skeptical of all of them.  But Eliot, whose unmarried union
with George Henry Lewes was an affront to polite society,
was of the type who insisted on believing in something.  Even
her later agnosticism had a kind of religious fervor to it.

As a girl, Eliot (born Mary Ann Evans, which she
preferred to spell Marian) underwent a narrow evangelical
education.  Predictably, she succumbed to it, at least for
a time.  As she matured, however, a subtler religiosity replaced the strenuous beliefs of her youth.  A true test of
her feelings came with the death of her father, whose lack
of kindness toward his devoted daughter is well known.  Mr.
Evans's final illness began late in 1848, notes Eliot's biographer.

> He lingered on five months longer with Mary
> Ann [sic] watching over him constantly, writing
> hurried little reports on every variation in his
> condition to her brothers and sisters.  None of
> them cared for him as she did.  It was no matter
> to her that the Waverley novels or her mother's
> silver forks would go to another.  She now had
> spiritual resources that ignored such trifles.  She
> had bought a copy of De Imitatione Christi by
> Thomas à Kempis, a new edition with quaint little
> woodcuts, which taught her--as it did Maggie Tul-
> liver--that true peace lay in resignation, in renun-
> ciation of self, an inner peace far deeper than any
> she had known at the height of her evangelical
> fervour, when she had enjoyed being taunted with
> the name of "saint."[1]

On February 9, 1849, during the worst days of her
father's illness, Eliot wrote her friend Sara Sophia Hennell
a letter that begins:  "My life is a perpetual nightmare--
always haunted by something to be done which I have never
the time or rather the energy to do. ... dear Father is very
uneasy and his moans distract me."  She goes on to discuss
other matters and then concludes, in a manner completely
different from that of her opening lines:  "I have at last the
most delightful 'de imitatione Christi' with quaint woodcuts.
One breathes a cool air as of cloisters in the book--it makes
one long to be a saint for a few months.  Verily its piety
has its foundations in the depth of the divine-human soul."[2]

Thomas à Kempis was born at Kempen, near Düssel-
dorf, in 1380 and died in 1471.  An Augustinian monk, he
wrote a number of devotional works, the best known of which
is The Imitation of Christ, once thought to be the work of
Jean Charlier de Gerson, a French theologian and Benedictine
monk.  The Imitation traces the gradual progress of the soul
toward perfection, which it attains through detachment from
the world and union with God.  Widely translated, The Imitation achieved and maintained a certain popularity not only
because of the obvious sincerity of its teachings but also because it represents, especially in modern times, an irrecov-
erable simplicity.[3]  That The Imitation had a transforming
effect on George Eliot is obvious from the effusive language
with which she describes the book's impact on the life of
Maggie Tulliver, the semiautobiographical heroine of The
Mill on the Floss.

The Imitation of Christ enters Maggie's life during
her adolescence.  No longer a child, but not yet an adult,
she is Freud's idea of a human being, a creature unconscious of its true desires, for "she could make dream-worlds
of her own but no dream-world would satisfy her now."4   All
she knows is that she is unhappy:

> She wanted some explanation of this hard, real
> life:  the unhappy-looking father, seated at the dull
> breakfast-table; the childish, bewildered mother;
> the little sordid tasks that filled the hours, or the
> more oppressive emptiness of weary, joyless lei-
> sure; the need of some tender demonstrative love;
> the cruel sense that [her brother] Tom didn't mind
> what she thought or felt, and that they were no
> longer playfellows together; the privation of all
> pleasant things that had come to her more than to
> others--she wanted some key that would enable her
> to understand, and in understanding endure, the
> heavy weight that had fallen on her young heart. 5

In her misery, she hopes that books will give her the answers
she wants ("If she had been taught 'real learning and wisdom,
such as great men knew,' she thought she should have held
the secret of life; if she had only books, that she might learn
for herself what wise men knew!"6).   Thomas à Kempis
could have told Maggie that she is wasting her time on hopes
like these, for The Imitation of Christ disdains such learning:

> At the Day of Judgment, we shall not be asked
> what we have read, but what we have done; not
> how eloquently we have spoken, but how holily we
> have lived.  Tell me, where are now all those
> Masters and Doctors whom you knew so well in
> their lifetime in the full flower of their learning?
> Other men now sit in their seats, and they are
> hardly ever called to mind.  In their lifetime they
> seemed of great account, but now no one speaks of
> them. 7

And indeed, the books she is able to put her hands
on are useless, with a single exception:

> Beauties of the Spectator, Rasselas, Economy of Hu-
> man Life, Gregory's Letters--she knew the sort of
> matter that was inside all these.  The Christian
> Year--that seemed to be a hymn-book, and she laid

it down again; but Thomas à Kempis--the name had
come across her in her reading, and she felt the
satisfaction which everyone knows, of getting some
ideas to attach to a name that strays solitary in
the memory.   She took up the little, old, clumsy
book with some curiosity; it had the corners turned
down in many places, and some hand, now forever
quiet, had made at certain passages strong pen-and-
ink marks, long since browned by time.   Maggie
turned from leaf to leaf and read where the quiet
hand pointed:  "Know that the love of thyself doth
hurt thee more than anything in the world. . . .   If
thou seekest this or that, and wouldst be here or
there to enjoy thy own will or pleasure, thou shalt
never be quiet nor free from care:  for in everything somewhat will be wanting, and in every place
there will be some that will cross thee. . . .   Both
above and below, which so ever way thou dost turn
thee, everywhere thou shalt find the Cross:  and
everywhere of necessity thou must have patience,
if thou wilt have inward peace, and enjoy an everlasting crown. . . .   If thou desire to mount unto this
height, thou must set out courageously, and lay the
axe to the root, that thou mayst pluck up and destroy that hidden inordinate inclination to thyself,
and unto all private and earthly good.   On this sin,
that a man inordinately love himself, almost all de-
pendeth, whatsoever is thoroughly to be overcome;
which evil being once overcome and subdued, there
will presently ensue great peace and tranquillity. . . .
It is but little thou sufferest in comparison of them
that have suffered so much, where so strongly
tempted, so grievously afflicted, so many ways
tried and exercised.   Thou oughtest therefore to
call to mind the more heavy sufferings of others,
that thou may the easier bear thy little adversities.
And if they seem not little unto thee, beware lest
thy impatience be the cause thereof. . . .   Blessed
are those ears that receive the whispers of the divine voice, and listen not to the whisperings of the
world.   Blessed are those ears which hearken not
unto the voice which soundeth outwardly, but unto
the Truth, which teacheth inwardly. . . ."[8]

   Why is The Imitation of Christ an exception, a useful
book amid all the useless ones that Maggie handles and dis-
cards?   The answer to this question is not to be found in the

excerpts from Thomas quoted above. There the language is hectoring and judgmental; knowing her readers, Eliot apparently skipped over the more esoteric passages and chose ones that, while calling to mind the asceticism and rigor of the monastic life, could still be reconciled with mainstream church teachings. However, the importance of The Imitation of Christ is not a doctrinal one. Unlike Rasselas and the other neoclassical books that Maggie rejects, The Imitation speaks to the spirit rather than the mind. It does not matter that Maggie is no scholar, and in fact her lack of scholarship seems to be a virtue: "She knew nothing of doctrines and systems, of mysticism and quietism, but this voice out of the far-off Middle Ages was the direct communication of a human soul's belief and experience, and came to Maggie as an unquestioned message."[9] From the title of Thomas's book, it is clear that Christ is less important as a giver of doctrines than as One to emulate, and a close examination of The Imitation reveals that the emphasis is on practical behavior within the context of ordinary life.

Early in The Imitation, there is a remarkable echo of Epictetus' Stoical dictum, "Live unknown." Thomas says, "Take delight in being unknown,"[10] a choice that, as we know from the various monistic thinkers studied in Chapter 1, entails a strenuous denial of the world's gaudy temptations. And indeed, the foremost theme of The Imitation seems to be the importance of a cultivated detachment, a rigorous avoidance of the temptation to wealth, fame, and success. The first sentence of the chapter "On Control of the Desires" reads: "Whenever a man desires anything inordinately, at once he becomes restless."[11] Later in the book, a reiteration of this theme recalls the language of Freud's little essay "On Transience": "Remember that all the things of this world are transitory. All things are passing, and yourself with them."[12]

A further elaboration of this idea is stern in tone, and it brings to mind the ascetic monism of the Egyptian Fathers and their Buddhist counterparts:

> Do you imagine that worldly men suffer little or nothing? Ask the most wealthy, and you will not find it so.
> But, you may say, they enjoy many pleasures, and follow their own desires; in this way they make light of any troubles. Yet, even if they enjoy whatever they desire, how long will this last? The

> rich of this world will vanish like smoke, and no
> memory of their past pleasures will remain. But
> even in their lifetime they do not enjoy them with-
> out bitterness, weariness, and fear, for the very
> things whence they derive their pleasures often
> carry with them the seeds of sorrow. And this is
> but just; for having sought and followed pleasures
> to excess, they may not enjoy them without shame
> and bitterness. Ah, how short-lived and false, how
> disorderly and base are all these pleasures! [13]

Of course, detachment is unobtainable as long as we
fail to acknowledge our own absence of self. "But if I hum-
ble myself and acknowledge my nothingness," says Thomas
in a direct address to Christ, "if I cast away all my self-
esteem and reduce myself to the dust that I really am, then
Your grace will come to me, and Your light will enter my
heart; thus will the last trace of self-esteem be engulfed in
the depth of my own nothingness, and perish forever." [14]
These lines suggest not only the ideas discussed in Chapter
1 but also the existentialist notion of the self as a bubble
without a center, an idea to be treated in more detail in
Chapter 6. How can a nothing be attracted to anything except through self-delusion?

When she discovers The Imitation of Christ, "Maggie
was still panting for happiness, and was in ecstasy because
she had found the key to it." [15] Her life is transformed:

> And it was by being brought within the long linger-
> ing of such a voice [as Thomas's] that Maggie, with
> her girl's face and unnoted sorrows, found an ef-
> fort and a hope that helped her through years of
> loneliness, making out a faith for herself without
> the aid of established authorities and appointed
> guides, for they were not at hand and her need
> was pressing. [16]

After a time, the change becomes discernible to others:

> That new inward life of hers, notwithstanding some
> volcanic upheavals of imprisoned passions, yet shone
> out in her face with a tender soft light that mingled
> itself as added loveliness with the gradually enriched
> colour and outline of her blossoming youth. Her
> mother felt the change in her with a sort of puzzled
> wonder that Maggie should be "growing up so good";

it was amazing that this once "contrairy" child was become so submissive, so backward to assert her own will. 17

It is, evident that Maggie has taken to heart the chapter in The Imitation entitled "How Sorrows Are to Be Borne Patiently," in which Thomas prays:

> Lord, because You were patient in Your life, in this respect especially fulfilling the command of Your Father, it is fitting that I, a wretched sinner, should bear myself patiently in accordance with Your will, and that, for the salvation of my soul, I should bear the burden of this corruptible life so long as You shall will. 18

Yet Maggie is young, and her efforts to shoulder the burden of life are unduly zealous. Dwellers in religious communities tell us that excess zeal is a danger, especially to the novice. Since Maggie is "making out a faith for herself without established authorities and appointed guides," and since she is prone to zealousness anyway, the danger is doubly great:

> From what you know of her [says the narrator to the reader], you will not be surprised that she threw some exaggeration and wilfulness, some pride and impetuosity, even into her self-renunciation; her own life was still a drama for her in which she demanded of herself that her part should be played with intensity. And so it came to pass that she often lost the spirit of humility by being excessive in the outward act; she often strove after too high a flight and came down with her poor little half-fledged wings dabbled in the mud. 19

Erring in one direction, Maggie is soon to err in the other: excessive in her adherence to the counsel of Thomas, she will be excessive in her neglect of it. In strangely prophetic terms, Thomas predicts Maggie's downfall:

> Alas, after a short meditation we break off, and do not make a strict examination of our lives. We do not consider where our affections really lie, nor are we grieved at the sinfulness of our whole life. Yet it was because of the wickedness of men that the Flood came upon the earth. 20

Floods abound in The Mill on the Floss, and in fact Maggie
will lose her life in one.

Maggie's problem is that she has the right advice but
not the experience on which to test it. Her real tests come
after she has read Thomas à Kempis, when its effect has already diminished. Hers is the mere universal unhappiness
of adolescence; had she experienced true sorrow and felt it
lessen under the benign influence of The Imitation of Christ,
she would have recognized the usefulness of its precepts and
clung to them more tightly. As it is, she lets down her
guard, whereas Thomas has already warned her:

> We need especially to be on our guard at the very
> outset of temptation, for then the Enemy may be
> more easily overcome, if he is not allowed to enter
> the gates of the mind: he must be repulsed at the
> threshold, as soon as he knocks. Thus the poet
> Ovid writes, "Resist at the beginning; the remedy
> may come too late."[21]

In Maggie's case, it would be more accurate to say that the
remedy has come too early.

Maggie's trials can be detailed quickly. First, she
falls in love with Philip Wakem, son of her father's enemy.
Then, her brother Tom forbids her to see Philip, thus cost-
ing her a normal relationship with her lover as well as straining the bond of affection between Maggie and Tom. Finally,
while maintaining a secret agreement with Philip she falls in
love with her cousin Lucy's fiancé, Stephen Guest, and he
falls in love with her. With all this muddle, it seems only
fit for Eliot to use water imagery to describe Maggie's di-
lemma. According to Eliot's pattern, the busy flow of life
is a river, while Maggie's increasingly rarer moments of
inner peace are a quiet pond. Thus, pondering her divided
affection for Philip and Stephen, Maggie thinks: "Was her
life to be always like this? Always bringing some new source
of inward strife? She heard confusedly the busy indifferent
voices around her and wished her mind could flow into that
easy, babbling current."[22] When Stephen presses his suit
and says it would be better for them to marry no matter how
much pain they cause others, "Maggie was silent. If it were
not wrong--if she were once convinced of that and need no
longer beat and struggle against this current, soft and yet
strong as the summer stream!"[23] Ironically, it is Lucy, the
cousin whom Maggie has betrayed, who uses water imagery

to contrast Maggie's quiet, solitary tendencies with the turbu-
lence of love.  Looking forward to an outing on the river with
the other young people, Lucy says:  " 'If the Floss were but a
quiet lake instead of a river, we should be independent of any
gentleman, for Maggie can row splendidly. ' "24

At this point the river that has been referred to metaphorically becomes a literal force in the narrative.  When
Lucy and Philip are prevented from going on the boat trip,
Stephen deliberately lets the boat drift so far downstream that
he and Maggie (who has been meditative and has failed to notice how far they have gone) will need several days to return
home by land and must therefore marry to avoid disgrace.
But Maggie will not marry Stephen, so her reputation dies.
She has not been mindful.  She meditated when she should
have exercised the awareness that is the fruit of meditation;
caught in the flow, she goes to a social death, which presages
her biological death, for at the book's end there is a real
flood, and Maggie drowns.

How strong is the current!  Yet despite the significance
of the water imagery, with its suggestion that life is a river
whose force is irresistible, The Mill on the Floss is often
read as a conventional morality tale, in which a scheming
heroine is killed as punishment for sins committed coldly and
deliberately.  Swinburne read the novel this way, for instance.
According to Ellen Moers,

> No such "abyss of cynicism" on the subject of fe-
> male character had been sounded by the wickedest
> of French novelists--not by Stendhal, Mérimée, or
> Laclos.  "My faith will not digest at once," [Swin-
> burne] wrote, "the first two volumes and the third
> volume of 'The Mill on the Floss'; my conscience
> or credulity has not enough gorge for such a gulp. "25

It could be that an analysis of "female character" by someone
with tastes as specialized as Swinburne's is questionable.
What defies belief is that, a hundred years later, the fem-
inist critic from whose essay I have lifted the Swinburne quotation describes Maggie in terms that are even more arch
and disapproving.  To Ellen Moers, The Mill on the Floss
is the story of "a sensitive, misunderstood child" who is not
to turn into "a mature woman of intellectual distinction and
wide ambition--a femme supérieure, like Mme de Staël or
George Eliot herself--but instead into a merely pretty and
dangerous flirt who steals a rich, good-looking suitor away

from her cousin Lucy. "[26]  Making much of Maggie's dark
hair, Moers asserts that "Maggie's convenient death in a
flood is designed to smooth over, both practically and mor-
ally, her ugly revenge on blondes in the person of 'dear little
Lucy.' "[27]

It is as though Maggie's lengthy effusions over The
Imitation of Christ were not there at all.  For all of its
emphasis on Maggie's spiritual striving, The Mill on the Floss
is read primarily as a love story, and not a very noble one
at that.  Maggie Tulliver is as misunderstood as Bartleby is,
and for the same reason--because she does not meet our cultural expectations.  To see The Mill on the Floss as a tale
in which the perpetrator of an "ugly revenge" gets her practical and moral comeuppance is to miss the connections between Eliot's novel and the age-old, universal monistic tradition that is its wellspring.  It would be hard to find a better
example of readers condemning a novel because it does not
answer to the requirements of their own narrow culture.  And
in addition to condemning the book, readers like Swinburne
and Moers are in fact rewriting it and leaving out the elements that do not fit.

It is unfair to chastise such readers to any great extent, however.  As we know, the problem with monism is its
tendency toward self-effacement; philosophies of passivity and
detachment do not call attention to themselves.  With respect
to The Mill on the Floss in particular, it must be admitted
that the lessons of Thomas à Kempis are useless.  Nothing
can save Maggie from the metaphorical river of passion that
disturbs her emotions, nothing can keep her from drowning
in the real one that claims her life.  One critic surmises that
Eliot may have intended to suggest that The Imitation of Christ
was merely a soothing book rather than a particularly helpful
one.  U. C. Knoepflmacher writes that

> George Eliot may well have been aware of Ernest
> Renan's influential essay on "L'Auteur de l'Imitation
> de Jésus Christ," in his Etudes d'Histoire Reli-
> gieuse (1857).  In his essay Renan views the author
> of the Imitation (whom he assumes to be the Bene-
> dictine Jean Gerson rather than Thomas à Kempis)
> much as Arnold regards the Carthusians in "Stanzas
> from the Grande Chartreuse."  As the "last voice
> of monachism," the book is too simple, too reac-
> tionary and uncurious ("to increase knowledge is to
> increase trouble"). [28]

But Eliot makes it clear that there is nothing insuffi-
cient about The Imitation of Christ, that the problem lies with
the youthful Maggie's inability to exercise Thomas's teachings
with equanimity. Religious thought that goes untested by the
exigencies of everyday life is meaningless, and even the most
faithful adepts have difficulty reconciling doctrine and practice.
Victorian fiction frequently deals with the uselessness of mere
knowledge, and for Maggie to suffer disgrace and death despite
her salvation is quite consistent with the strain of pessimism
found in the novels of Hardy and others. It is not knowledge
that Maggie lacks but the experience that would allow her to
test what she has learned and devise ways to apply it. As
Knoepflmacher says, "It is Maggie's own experience ... which
must be her teacher, even if that experience leads her to
death."[29]

# THE PORTRAIT OF A LADY

"The ladies will save us."

In <u>Don Quixote</u>, Sancho Panza tells his master a story involving a fisherman who must ferry a flock of goats across a river, one at a time. "Keep an account of the goats which the fisherman is taking over, your worship, for if you lose count of one the story will end, and it won't be possible for me to tell you another word of it." But when the Don realizes that Sancho, like the fisherman, is going to transport each goat separately, he interrupts impatiently and says, "Take it that they are all across, and do not go on coming and going like that, or you will never get them all over in a year." Sancho asks, "How many have got over so far?" and Don Quixote replies, "How the devil should I know?" His story ruined, Sancho Panza admonishes his master: "There now, didn't I tell you to keep a good count? Well, there's an end of the story. God knows there's no going on with it now."[1]

The kind of fiction that Cervantes satirizes in this passage is the kind that James deplored as well; it is fiction written according to the two-and-two-make-four system (as James called it in a scornful letter to his brother, William). Indeed, James seems so implacably opposed to heavily plotted fiction, especially in his later work, that the novice reader sometimes makes the mistake of seeing James as an exemplum of the disembodied intellect. Yet as T. S. Eliot remarked, James's most telling characteristic is "his mastery over, his baffling escape from ideas; a mastery and escape which are perhaps the last test of a superior intelligence. He had a mind so fine that no idea could violate it."[2] Puzzling and often misinterpreted willfully, this remark does not have to be taken to mean that Eliot thought James stupid. As Philip Rieff says,

By "idea," Eliot meant ideology, I think:
ideas that excited minds acquire when the
leased from patient thought.... In his fa...ous ex-
coriation of a Trollope novel, James wrote: "Our
great objection to 'The Belton Estate' is that we
seem to be reading a work written for children, a
work prepared for minds unable to think, a work
below the apprehension of the average man or woman,
'The Belton Estate' is a stupid book ... essentially,
organically stupid. It is without a single idea. It
is utterly incompetent to the primary function of a
book of whatever nature, to suggest thought" [Rieff's
italics]. Perfectly said. Much of what passes for
"Liberation" writing and chat, nowadays, is below
the apprehension of the average man or woman, intended for the expanding market of educated fools,
the Sniffpecks of our anti-culture. [3]

Returning to T. S. Eliot's comment, Rieff says that "here is
the trouble with us, and with the masses we educate: our
minds are too easily violated by ideas. We paste ideas on
our foreheads, in order to follow them."[4]

Rieff makes these remarks in the essay "Fellow Teachers," which is in fact about pedagogy and not literature.
Rieff sees in Eliot's description of James "a hint of the perfect teacher." He sees James himself as a writer and thinker
who "offers one splendid example of complex, unprogressive
teaching, unaddicted precisely to ideas."[5] Like other great
teachers, James appears at a time of crisis. Some writers
describe James's world and his response to it in language
that is highly charged and sometimes nearly hysterical:

James lived in a time, just preceding World War
I, when the fabric began to fray, if not unravel.
His fictions are bastions, increasingly desperate,
increasingly sophisticated, therefore increasingly
wordy, against that unraveling, against the wrench-
ing of bourgeois clarity. James believed--by God,
would believe--in the ability, in the very right of
the individual to perceive, to see, to understand,
and to accept responsibility for his or her vision.
His novels are filled with fine objects as if they
were, themselves, museums.

When he walked out of the refuge of his study into

the world and looked about him, he saw a place
of torment, where creatures of prey perpetually
thrust their claws into the quivering flesh of the
doomed, defenceless children of light. He had the
abiding comfort of an inner certainty ... that the
children of light had an eternal advantage; he was
aware to the finest fibre of his being that the "poor
sensitive gentlemen" he so numerously treated pos-
sessed a treasure that would outlast all the glitter-
ing paste of the world and the flesh; he knew that
nothing in life mattered compared with spiritual
decency.

The first quotation is from a paper a student wrote for a
course of mine several years ago; the second is from the
memoirs of James's amanuensis, Theodora Bosanquet, to
whom a good deal of his later writing was dictated. [6] Separate in terms of time as well as sensibility, these two excerpts capture nonetheless an essentially melodramatic preoccupation of James.

In The Melodramatic Imagination: Balzac, Henry
James, Melodrama, and the Mode of Excess, Peter Brooks
explains that melodrama as a genre was born in the context
of the French Revolution and its aftermath and that it seeks
new definitions in a world without fixed values. [7] Tragedy, a
pre-Revolutionary genre, seeks resolutions for moral problems that are easily apprehended within the framework of a
shared value system. In contrast, melodrama can only attempt to express all, to articulate everything.

In one sense, this garrulous genre is perfect for the
nineteenth century. It is no accident that the success of
melodramatic fiction is tied to the success of the middle
class. As the middle class grew, so did its curiosity about
the other classes, and the novel prospered because it has
traditionally served as an inexpensive source of information
about the rich and the poor. A basic recipe for successful
fiction is to (1) tell the middle-class reader how the rich
(or poor) live and (2) reinforce the reader's notion of his or
her superiority to the rich (or poor). A mass of detail, a
dash of morality.

The difference is that James gives the detail but with-
holds the comforting morality. It is a commonplace that
James is an "ambiguous" writer, but the adjective itself has
two meanings. It can mean doubtful and uncertain, or it can

mean susceptible to more than one interpretation. The second definition is the one that applies to James's writing, and it is one that I shall explore in greater detail before concluding these introductory remarks. In the meantime, perhaps it suffices to say that, in a way, James is easier to read than we think. He is easy to read because the reader needs no preconceptions. James is not "about" anything. As Philip Rieff says, he is "unaddicted precisely to ideas." Or, as Samuel Beckett writes in his little book on Proust, "the quality of language is more important than any system of ethics or aesthetics."[8]

Norman O. Brown says that "Finnegans Wake is not about anything, it is that thing itself."[9] The same is true of Moby-Dick, which certainly is not about a whale. The same is true of Swann's Way. And in the midpoint of his career, James's fictions stop being about things and become things. The American, for example, is about Christopher Newman, its hero. But The Ambassadors, written a quarter of a century later, is not about Lambert Strether: it is Lambert Strether and Strether's world, not described but painstakingly created. On the whole, then, and regardless of what well-intended readers have said, James's fiction is not about Swedenborgianism or pragmatism or spiritualism or the teachings of Josiah Royce. A James novel is not a subject. It is an act--an act of consciousness.

In Chapter 26 of The Wings of the Dove, Merton Densher is thinking of the love that he shares with Kate Croy and how he discerns in it "the whole soft breath of consciousness meeting and promoting consciousness."[10] Consciousness meeting and promoting consciousness: the perfect act of love, of reading, of teaching. This is precisely the concern of the esoteric masters and teachers discussed in the first chapter of this study. An Oriental proverb says that "to enjoy the benefits of Providence is wisdom; to make others enjoy them is virtue."[11] James himself once wrote that the novel deals with "the whole human consciousness."[12] More accurately, the business of the novel is with the consciousness as it interacts with other consciousnesses, as it meets and (it is to be hoped) promotes them.

According to poet Todd Gitlin, "Consciousness is reparation / for the primal theft."[13] In fact, there is a biographical explanation for James's obsession with consciousness. As a child, James realized that he could never compete successfully in the external world with his older brother,

William. In <u>A Small Boy and Others</u>, Henry writes that
William "had gained such an advantage of me in his sixteen
months' experience of the world before mine began that I
never for all the time of childhood and youth in the least
caught up with him or overtook him." William, like Esau,
the first son of the Old Testament story, was the active one.
Henry, like Jacob, the second son, was the stay-at-home, a
dweller in tents. William became a scientist, husband, father. Henry found it more natural to cultivate the self. [14]

In the same poem, Todd Gitlin asserts that consciousness "is the necessary / shield against the flux of things."
One of the most searing experiences of James's youth was
the death of his beloved cousin Minny Temple, but in a letter
to his mother he wrote that "the more I think of her the more
perfectly satisfied I am to have her translated from this
changing realm of fact to the sturdy realm of thought." [15] In
<u>The Portrait of a Lady</u>, James reverses the circumstances
by having his surrogate, Ralph Touchett, die of consumption
(as Minny did) while the heroine, Isabel Archer, is advised
to use her consciousness as a necessary shield against the
flux of things. " 'You won't lose me--you'll keep me,' " says
Ralph to Isabel from his deathbed. " 'Keep me in your heart;
I shall be nearer to you than I've ever been.' " [16]

Late in 1900, his friend Morton Fullerton asked James
what had been the "port" from which he had taken sail, the
point of departure of his life and art. James replied: " 'The
port from which I set out was, I think, that of <u>the essential
loneliness of my life</u>.' " [17] Students who think of James as a
heavyweight are sometimes surprised to find a colloquial, if
rarefied, tone in his later writings, many of which were
dictated to Theodora Bosanquet and other amanuenses. Even
his private papers, his journals and notebooks, are conver-
sational in tone, as though someone were being addressed.
With whom then was James speaking? In a sense, his writings may be thought of as a long conversation with the self,
a refinement and elaboration of his own consciousness that
compensated for his essential loneliness in a way that no
wife or child or other domestic society could. A novelist
must begin in loneliness, in communion with self. Anyone
who has ever talked at length with novelists know that they
often complain bitterly about this self-isolating aspect of their
craft. But from the lone self comes the multiple consciousnesses that constitute the novelist's world.

The significance of this essential loneliness to James's

art is nowhere more clearly seen than in his decision in 1897 to move from his flat in London to Lamb House, Rye, Sussex. As Leon Edel writes:

> Out of the hours of Rye's solitude, there took shape and were written within four years the three last novels, the summit of his creation. It was as if his years of ceaseless wandering and dwelling in cities had prepared him for this final communion with himself, a reforging out of memory and lone-liness of his visions of the civilization absorbed during forty years of cosmopolitan life. [18]

The novels are The Ambassadors, The Wings of the Dove, and The Golden Bowl, James's acknowledged masterpieces, works that are coincidental with James's deliberate remove from society for the "final communion with himself." The decision to buy Lamb House came during the most harrowing period in James's life, a time when almost all of his energy went into an unsuccessful and ultimately humiliating attempt to have his plays produced on the London stage; the subtitle Leon Edel chose for the volume of the James biography that covers the years 1895-1900 is The Treacherous Years. But out of that torment came the decision not only to change dwellings but to cultivate through self-discipline the mindful-ness and awareness that would enable him to produce his best work. And to do this he found it necessary to forswear the garish temptations of the city.

That James's preoccupation with consciousness grew over the years can be seen in his increased use of the past perfect tense in narration. Hisayoshi Watanabe juxtaposes passages from two novels, Roderick Hudson (1876) and The Golden Bowl (1904) to show the effect of this change. The passages are quite similar; in each "a sudden resolution impels one character to destroy a work of art in the pres-ence of another, and a third character is introduced, sur-prised, to the scene." [19] In Roderick Hudson, the past tense is used typically, as the normal tense of narration:

> "I want to begin," [Roderick] cried, "and I can't make a better beginning than this! Good-bye, Mr. Barnaby Striker!" He strode across the room, seized a hammer that lay at hand, and before Row-land could interfere, in the interest of art if not of morals, dealt a merciless blow upon Mr. Striker's skull. The bust cracked into a dozen pieces, which

toppled with a great crash upon the floor. Rowland
relished neither the destruction of the image nor
his companion's expression in working it, but as
he was about to express his displeasure the door
opened and gave passage to a fresh-looking girl.
She came in with a rapid step and startled face,
as if she had been alarmed by the noise. Meeting
the heap of the shattered clay and the hammer in
Roderick's hand, she gave a cry of horror. Her
voice died away as she saw Rowland was a stranger,
but she had sounded her reproach. "Why, Roderick,
what on earth have you done?"

There is only one use of the past perfect tense in this passage, near the end: "she had sounded." By way of contrast,
there is this passage from The Golden Bowl:

"Well then, if it's because of this--!" And
Fanny Assingham, who had been casting about her
and whose inspiration decidedly had come, raised
the cup in her two hands, raised it positively above
her head, and from under it, solemnly, smiled at
the Princess as a signal of intention. So for an
instant, full of her thought and her act, she held
the precious vessel, and then, with due note taken
of the margin of the polished floor, bare, fine and
hard in the embrasure of her window, she dashed
it boldly to the ground, where she had the thrill of
seeing it, with the violence of the crash, lie shattered. She had flushed with the force of her effort,
as Maggie had flushed with wonder at the sight, and
this high reflection in their faces was all that passed
between them for a minute more. After which,
"Whatever you meant by it--and I don't want to know
now--has ceased to exist," Mrs. Assingham said.
"And what in the world, my dear, did you mean
by it?"--that sound, as at the touch of a spring,
rang out as the first effect of Fanny's speech. It
broke upon the two women's absorption with a sharp-
ness almost equal to the smash of the crystal, for
the door of the room had been opened by the Prince
without their taking heed. [20]

As in Roderick Hudson, the act of smashing the artwork is
reported in the past tense. However, the sentences that pre-
cede and follow the description of the act in this passage use
the past perfect tense. The emphasis in Roderick Hudson is

on simple action. But the emphasis in The Golden Bowl is on action perceived, weighed, judged, made more than itself through the enhancing power of consciousness.

The foregoing is somewhat technical, but after all, a James novel is but an elaborate and refined version of what any novel is. The lines from Epictetus that Sterne chose as the epigraph of Tristram Shandy may be translated thus: "It is not actions, but opinions concerning actions, which disturb men." This is the stuff of the novel: not the temporal and spatial phenomena of the fictional world--the actions--and certainly not opinions themselves (though James is sometimes accused of being concerned with opinions only), but opinions concerning actions. James is simply fulfilling the promise of Epictetus in his preoccupation with consciousness.

Once James's intent is grasped, we can attribute one idiosyncrasy after another to this preoccupation. In the preface to The Portrait of a Lady, James writes:

> "Place the centre of the subject in the young woman's own consciousness," I said to myself, "and you get as interesting and as beautiful a difficulty as you could wish. Stick to that--for the centre; put the heaviest weight into that scale, which will be so largely the scale of her relation to herself. Make her only interested enough, at the same time, in the things that are not herself, and this relation needn't fear to be too limited."[21]

It is " 'the things that are not herself' " that meet and promote the consciousness of James's heroine. Throughout the novel, Isabel Archer is surrounded by various "satellites": Ralph Touchett, Lord Warburton, Caspar Goodwood, Gilbert Osmond, and so on. In the preface, James cautions himself to " 'press least hard ... on the consciousness of your heroine's satellites.' "[22] The Portrait of a Lady is a novel of conspiracy; no wonder that James uses the singular collective noun "consciousness" instead of the expected plural. In James's scale, the collective consciousness of the satellites is balanced against the single consciousness of Isabel. Consciousness meeting and promoting consciousness: these are the terms of James's plan for his novel, his preoccupation.

As in plan, so in practice. When Isabel, who is bookish and provincial, first sees Lord Warburton, she exclaims: " 'Oh, I hoped there would be a lord; it's just like a novel!' "[23]

This statement suggests several things: (1) it indicates where her consciousness has been--between book covers, for the most part; (2) it shows where her consciousness is now--on the brink of expansion; and (3) it suggests how far her consciousness has to go. Isabel's expanding consciousness is what holds the novel together. Occupation--James's actual writing of the novel--coalesces with preoccupation.

There is a genuine sense of challenge in James's preface to The Portrait of a Lady. " 'See, at all events, what can be done,'" James counsels himself. [24] The challenge is to write a novel of character rather than a novel of incident. To James, incident is a means rather than an end. In "The Art of Fiction," he writes: "What is incident but the illustration of character? What is ... a novel that is not of character? What else do we seek and find in it?"[25] In Theory of Fiction: Henry James, James E. Miller, Jr., refers to "the recurring complaint that nothing much ever happens in a James novel." The fact is, writes Miller, "that such complaints arise because the reader or critic has focused his attention in the wrong place--on the events themselves rather than on the dramatized consciousness interacting with the events."[26] In his criticism, James probably wrote "more frequently about character than any other element" and he "organized his own fictions as dramas of consciousness rather than as complications of actions."[27] Frequently, what could have happened in a James novel already has: Madame Merle has already had Pansy by Osmond (The Portrait of a Lady); Peter Quint and Miss Jessel have already died and seem to have returned as ghosts (The Turn of the Screw); Chad Newsome has already established his relationship with Madame de Vionnet (The Ambassadors). What matters is the effort made by Isabel Archer, the governess, and Lambert Strether to puzzle out these situations and decide what to do about them. That is what is meant by the phrase "drama of consciousness."

"Consciousness" may strike the reader as an abstraction, but a little further reading in James suggests that, as with the esoteric masters discussed in Chapter 1 of this study, consciousness is nothing more than mindfulness or awareness and is therefore linked to the idea of clear sight. "Probably one of the two most important words in James's critical vocabulary was impressions," writes Miller. "The other was consciousness. The connection between the two is obvious-- the consciousness is the storehouse of one's impressions."[28] In "The Art of Fiction," James takes issue with a critic who had asserted that a young lady who has grown up in a quiet country village should avoid descriptions of the military life. To the contrary, such a young lady may tackle any subject she pleases, says James, as long as she is "a damsel upon whom nothing is lost." And a page later, he advises another hypothetical writer to "'try to be one of the people on whom nothing is lost!'"[29]

The organ of sight was most important to James. In a journal entry dated July 25, 1885, the novelist Violet Paget wrote concerning a recent visit from James: "He came to see me again yesterday afternoon. He says his plan through life has been never to lose an opportunity of seeing anything of any kind; he urges me to do the same."[30] In his biography of James, Leon Edel notes a passage in The Ambassadors that stresses the importance of seeing. In the well-known scene in Gloriani's garden, Strether is addressing Little Bilham (quoted in Edel):

> "Live all you can; it's a mistake not to. It doesn't so much matter what you do in particular," he tells Bilham, "so long as you have your life...." Later, Little Bilham will change the speech slightly. He will remind Strether that he had said, "See all you can." Strether does not contradict him. Seeing is accordingly equated with living.[31]

Monistic literature is filled with references to sight. For instance, one of the sayings of the Desert Fathers is: "The monk should be all eye, like the cherubim and sera-phim."[32] This is not to say that James is a Christian or even an especially religious author, of course, because the emphasis in monistic philosophies as well as in the writings of Henry James is on the here and now, what it is and what to make of it. And in any case, the disposition toward clear sight no doubt precedes any moral or aesthetic activity. In A Small Boy and Others, James recalls that his earliest memory was a highly visual one: the "admirable aspect of the Place and the Colonne Vendôme" in Paris, a view "framed by the clear window" of the carriage in which he rode. In her critical study Henry James and the Visual Arts, Viola Hopkins Winner notes that the scene is remembered as a picture in a frame. The boy in long clothes was father to James "the observer-artist, passionately involved yet objective and detached."[32]

A passage from The American symbolizes the impor-

tance of sight in James. Valentin and Newman are walking
through the Louvre when they see Mademoiselle Noémie, the
ambitious little copyist, who has paused to study two ladies
who are dressed in a style far beyond her means.

> She was not at work; her palette and brushes had
> been laid down beside her, her hands were folded
> in her lap, and she was leaning back in her chair
> and looking intently at two ladies on the other side
> of the hall, who, with their backs turned to her,
> had stopped before one of the pictures. These la-
> dies were apparently persons of high fashion; they
> were dressed with great splendour, and their long
> silken trains and furbelows were spread over the
> polished floor. It was at their dresses Mademoi-
> selle Noémie was looking, though what she was
> thinking of I am unable to say. [33]

What a richness of pictures within pictures: a narrator is
looking at two men who are looking at a young girl who is
looking at two ladies who are looking at a picture within a
great hall of pictures ("the long gallery of the Italian masters") within the great pictorial museum itself within one of
the most visually striking cities in the world, Paris.

Yet the richness can be baffling, the prolixity disturbing. Life is more comfortable when there is less to see and
consider; most of us wear blinders well. What then are we
to do with a melodramatist who tries to express everything,
a deliberately ambiguous writer whose works can be read in
different and even conflicting ways? Henry Adams once la-
mented that "Henry James had not yet taught the world to read
a volume for the pleasure of seeing the lights of his burning-
glass turned on the alternate sides of the same figure."[34]
James will never be a best-selling author, of course. But
what is surprising is that so many of the classic critical studies of James see his ambiguity as a negative quality. Two
essays that are frequently cited are Yvor Winters's "Maule's
Well, or Henry James and the Relation of Morals to Manners"
and Edmund Wilson's "The Ambiguity of Henry James."[35]
Winters deals with the fact that James's moral sense is in-
consistent with "the ethical systems of the Roman Catholic
and Anglo-Catholic Churches"--not a great problem for most
readers, I think.[36] Wilson, on the other hand, is concerned
with James's intellectual inconsistency, although the two ap-
pendices to Wilson's essay, in which he changes and then re-
changes his mind about the ghosts in The Turn of the Screw,

suggest that inconsistency is less a Jamesian problem than a Wilsonian one, if, indeed, it is a problem at all.

No contemporary discussion of ambiguity, Jamesian or otherwise, can fail to mention Wayne Booth, whose remarks in The Rhetoric of Fiction are instructive, although in one respect they seem to be contradictory. One of his points is that ambiguity in and of itself is not necessarily bad, although it may come into conflict with some other aspect of a given work. [37]  The problem, however, is that Booth treats entire works as "ambiguous," whereas (as he himself admits) most complex art is ambiguous in certain ways but not in others. For instance, The Turn of the Screw, the bête noire of Booth, Wilson, and most of the other antis, is ambiguous in its epistemological concern (whether or not the ghosts are real) and yet quite direct in its treatment of the moral issue (the question of what the governess should do). [38]

After a while, discussions of this nature tend to become as vague and gassy as James's fiction is to his detractors.  Neither Winters nor Wilson nor Booth gives much attention to an aspect of James's craft that would provide some stepping-stones through the fog.  I am thinking of James's choice of images.  There are two images in particular that need to be examined, images that, far from suggesting ambiguity in the negative sense, indicate instead an almost geometric regularity in the works themselves as well as in the mind of the author who created them.

The first image is that of the medal, and it is consistent with James's view (and Freud's, to go back to Chapter 1) that there is more to what we see than the surface.  When, in a letter, for example, James refers to James Russell Lowell's "double existence--the American and the English sides of his medal," he invites the reader to look beyond the surface of Lowell's ostensibly American character and to see "the alternate sides of the same figure," as Henry Adams would say. [39]  An example of the use of the medal image to define a fictional character is seen in the description of Gilbert Osmond, who, on his first appearance in The Portrait of a Lady, is likened to a "fine gold coin," an "elegant complicated medal." [40]  Osmond's medal, like Lowell's has two sides:  the first is characterized by the elegance that makes Osmond attractive to Isabel Archer, whereas the second reveals the cold tyranny of which Isabel learns after it is too late.  Later, a version of the same image is used by Osmond to characterize Isabel.

> What could be a happier gift in a companion than a
> quick, fanciful mind which saved one repetitions and
> reflected one's thought on a polished, elegant sur-
> face? Osmond hated to see his thought reproduced
> literally--that made it look stale and stupid; he pre-
> ferred it to be freshened in the reproduction even
> as "words" by music. His egotism had never taken
> the crude form of desiring a dull wife; this lady's
> intelligence was to be a silver plate, not an earthen
> one--a plate that he might heap up with ripe fruits,
> to which it would give a decorative value, so that
> talk might become for him a sort of served dessert.
> He found the silver quality in this perfection in
> Isabel; he could tap her imagination with his knuckle
> and make it ring. [41]

And just as Osmond has a hidden side, so does Isabel. She
is not a showy plate to be rung at Osmond's behest; her actions in the final chapter make it clear that she is much more
than the passive object that Osmond wants her to be.

That James intended his fictions to be representations
of life's complexities is evident from his frequent reliance
on the medal image in his critical prefaces. For instance,
in writing about life as it is seen only from the limited perspective of a given social class, James refers to the "state
of the medal with its right face accidentally turned down."[42]
In a similar passage, he discusses the different meanings that
a particular state of affairs may have for different characters;
here he speaks of "that bright hard medal, of so strange an
alloy, one face of which is somebody's right and ease and the
other somebody's pain and wrong."[43] James also uses the
image of the medal to describe any given work of fiction
whatsoever: "Could I but make my medal hang free, its
obverse and its reverse, its face and its back, would beau-
tifully become optional for the spectator."[44] This superb
imagistic representation of the novelist's intent is faithful to
the necessarily ambiguous nature of both life and realistic
fiction. Elsewhere, James notes that the "muddled state too
is one of the very sharpest of the realities."[45] In point of
fact, James's writings are seldom so ambiguous as to be
"muddled." Rather, his writings simply indicate his willing-
ness and ability to see both sides of an issue or character.

As we have seen, James's freely hanging medal spins
a little too quickly for such critics as Winters, Wilson, and
Booth. But others have used James's view of the doubleness

of things as the basis for their own interpretations of his
work.   Philip Rahv, for example, finds a doubleness in the
themes of James, which he attributes to James's view of
his experiences as both ordeal and inspiration.   Thus, says
Rahv, "the 'great world' is corrupt [in James], yet it represents an irresistible goal."[46]   And Dorothea Krook writes
"that, in Henry James's total vision, the sense of the grim-
ness and bitterness of human life is inseparably fused with
the sense of its beauty and blessedness; that neither cancels
out the other; and that the ambiguity is intended to express
this experience of their permanent, inseparable fusion."[47]

How clear it is that to James the doubleness of things,
as suggested by the image of the medal, is basic even to
those fictional situations that are not described by the image
itself.   Isabel Archer must decide whether Gilbert Osmond
is a good prospect for marriage or not (The Portrait of a
Lady); Lambert Strether must decide whether Chad Newsome
has been corrupted or improved by his relationship with Madame de Vionnet (The Ambassadors); the governess must decide whether the ghosts that menace her charges are real or
imaginary (The Turn of the Screw); Hyacinth Robinson must
decide whether his political friends are sincere or hypocritical (The Princess Casamassima); Verena Tarrant must decide
whether Basil Ransom represents freedom or tyranny to her
(The Bostonians); and so on.   In each case, the image of the
medal can be used to describe the basic situation.   It "hangs
free," as James would say, and presents its different sides
alternately.

A second image employed by James is an even subtler
representation of the ambiguity of life and fiction.   The image
of the medal suggests the essential doubleness of things; its
philosophical premise is that surface realities are not the
only ones.   The second image, that of the circle, accepts
this premise and develops its implications in a way that the
relatively simple image of the medal cannot.   One typical
use of the circle in James involves characters who find themselves in difficult situations.   These characters are described
as "turning round," metaphorically circling or else revolving
within their situations in order to view and understand them
fully.   Such a character is the governess in The Turn of the
Screw, who, after dismissing Flora and Mrs. Grose in order
to devote all of her attention to the redemption of Miles, re-
flects on the difficulty of her task and remarks that "it was
a tighter place still than I had yet turned round in."[48]   In
The Portrait of a Lady, Isabel Archer is awaiting the arrival

of the importunate Caspar Goodwood; she fears a scene, and
the reader is told that she literally moves "in a vain circle."[49]
Rose Armiger of The Other House begs a similarly importunate young man:   " 'I'm only asking you again, as I've asked
you already, to be patient with me--to let me, at such a critical hour, turn round.' "   Later, the situation is reversed;
the pursuer becomes the pursued, and it is Rose who is on
the offensive.   The reaction of the startled young gentleman
is one of "instinctive retreat from being carried by assault,
and he had the effect ... of revolving blindly around her."[50]
In The Wings of the Dove, Merton Densher considers the futility of trying to prevent Maud Lowder from learning of his
secret engagement to Kate Croy, and he realizes that

> it was impossible to keep Mrs. Lowder out of their
> scheme.   She stood there too close to it and too
> solidly; it had to open a gate, at a given point, ...
> to take her in.   And she came in, always, while
> they sat together rather helplessly watching her,
> as in a coach-and-four; she drove round their pros-
> pect as the principal lady at the circus drives round
> the ring, and she stopped the coach in the middle to
> alight with majesty. [51]

Possibly the best known of these circular movements
occurs in Book Second of The Golden Bowl, which opens with
an image that represents Maggie Verver's "consciousness of
a recent change in her life."   It is the elaborate figure of a
pagoda, which suggests to Maggie her majestic and, as of
late, somewhat distant husband, Prince Amerigo.   The pagoda
is located "at the very centre of the garden of her life," and
she walks "round and round" it, wondering how to approach
an object so formidable.   She realizes the need for careful
reflection rather than a more aggressive approach, so she
encircles the pagoda cautiously before venturing "a tap or
two" upon "one of the rare porcelain plates."[52]

Just as the governess, Isabel, Rose, Maud, Maggie,
and the other characters tend to circle around aspects of life
that strike them as ambiguous, so the writer, and eventually
the reader, will examine the complex fictional subject from
all sides, hoping to grasp its complexity.   James makes this
abundantly clear in his critical prefaces when he refers  to
the "planned rotation of aspects" of a particular work (in this
case "The Reverberator"); or when he describes his blueprint
for The Awkward Age as a central object surrounded by a
circle of lamps, "the function of each of which would be to

light with all due intensity one of its aspects"; or when he
refers to the short story entitled "The Two Faces" as the
"example of the turn of the whole coach and pair in the con-
tracted court."[53]

Indeed, the concept of circularity is central to James's
critical theory.  Of the various terms that James applies to
his work, one of the most frequently used is "roundness" or
a variation thereof:  thus, in reference to the writing of The
Turn of the Screw, James notes that "the thing was to aim
at ... roundness," just as the thing to avoid was the "long
and loose, the copious, the various, the endless, where,
dramatically speaking, roundness is quite sacrificed...."[54]
And the concept is applied to other works that James considered successful:  "The Reverberator," for instance, is a
"little rounded drama"; "The Point of View" is a "little
rounded composition"; and The Spoils of Poynton has a "certain assured appearance of roundness and felicity."[55]  Finally,
The Ambassadors, which James considered the "most propor-
tioned of his productions" and a "structure reared with an
'architectural' competence," is characterized by a "superior
roundness" as well.[56]

Lama Anagarika Govinda writes that "the Eastern way
of thinking ... consists in a circling round the object of contemplation ... a many-sided, i.e., multi-dimensional impression formed from the superimposition of single impressions
from different points of view."[57]  This is a precise expression of James's intent in much of his fiction; it recalls rather
literally James's plan for The Awkward Age, the subject of
which would be at the center of a circle of lamps that are
turned on one by one.

But there is nothing exclusively Eastern about circles.
Emily Dickinson writes, "Success in Circuit lies" and "My
Business is Circumference."[58]  And when T. S. Eliot says,
"We shall not cease from exploration / And the end of all
our exploring / Will be to arrive where we started / And
know the place for the first time," he is saying not only that
we get lost but also that we need to get lost.[59]

To primitive and sophisticated peoples alike, the way
of the world is the circular way; to move in a straight line
is to violate the natural order.  The Sioux holy man Black
Elk says,

Everything an Indian does is in a circle, and that

> is because the power of the world always works in
> circles, and everything tries to be round. In the
> old days when we were a strong and happy people,
> all our power came to us from the sacred hoop of
> the nation, and so long as the hoop was unbroken
> the people flourished. [60]

To Emerson, "the eye is the first circle; the horizon which
it forms is the second; and throughout nature this primary
figure is repeated without end. It is the highest emblem in
the cipher of the world."[61]

In The Cycle of American Literature, a historical-
critical study with a circular title of its own, Robert E.
Spiller reminds us that the "back-trail" leads to the heart
of the American experience.

> There were many who followed Mark Twain into
> a vigorous acceptance of the expanding continent
> and the expanding world of the modern mind, but
> there were also many who reacted against all that
> the West called for and all that the Industrial Rev-
> olution and the new science demanded. By 1890
> two roads of future development in American litera-
> ture were clearly marked: the road that led to an
> open acceptance of nature and of things as they are,
> and the road that led inward to an exploration of
> the consciousness, to tradition, to restraint, and
> to concern for form. In an earlier day Poe and
> Hawthorne had in one way or another followed this
> second road, and in a later day it was to be fol-
> lowed by T. S. Eliot and Faulkner. This was the
> "back-trail" in a deeper sense than that in which
> Hamlin Garland used the term, yet it was somehow
> associated with the Eastward look and the search
> for tradition. Un-American as it often seemed,
> American literature could never have matured with-
> out it, could never have become more than a series
> of reports from the moving frontier. [62]

One hopes that in the present day readers do not have to be
told that "introspective writers like Poe, Emily Dickinson,
and Henry James were as much products of American culture
as were Whitman and Mark Twain," but Spiller does come
very close to the subject matter of the present study when
he reminds us that the tendency toward monism and quietism
that manifests itself in the works of cautious and "circular"

thinkers is just as valid as the dualism and activism that characterizes the writings of the more aggressive and goal-oriented types. [63]

Yet an equally emphatic theme of the present study is that the monist is necessarily a dualist (though not the other way around). One must choose, make decisions, act; even to vow silence and enter a monastery is dualistic. When does one stop circling, then? At what point should the circle be entered? These questions underline any contemplative activity and warn that right action is the end product of meditation, not masturbatory self-absorption. Richard Hocks, one of James's most sensitive critics, writes: "You ought not distinguish where you cannot divide ... [but] you sometimes must distinguish where you cannot divide, for fear of never grasping the unifying experience." [64] Good advice for literary critics, these words recall the often paradoxical necessity for both action and contemplation in the lives of most of us.

James's The Portrait of a Lady is a book-length study of the interplay of action and contemplation and the effect of this interplay on the developing consciousness of a young woman, Isabel Archer. Like the enlightened shoemaker, Isabel is both ordinary and extraordinary at one and the same time. Money and marriage are the themes of her story, just as they are the themes of countless other fictions. The genius of James enables her story to touch our lives as well, however, rather than simply titillate our shabbier instincts. To paraphrase Melville, the discerning reader stands hand in hand with Isabels the world over, "and one shock of recognition runs the whole circle round." [65]

★

"To be rich was a virtue," thinks Isabel Archer, "because it was to be able to do, and ... to do could only be sweet." [66] In a capitalist society, money buys freedom for those who cannot have it any other way. This was nowhere more true than for women in the nineteenth century. Isabel's cousin Ralph Touchett speculates on her future and wonders "what was she going to do with herself? This question was irregular, for with most women one had no occasion to ask it. Most women did with themselves nothing at all; they waited, in attitudes more or less gracefully passive, for a man to come that way and furnish them with a destiny." [67] Hence, the special quality of Isabel's character. As F. R. Leavis puts it, "An American heiress, merely because she is an American heiress, is a Princess, and such a Princess as is to be conceived as a supreme moral value."68

There is no doubt that James saw Isabel's freedom as a "supreme moral value," which is why he tantalizes her with both real and counterfeit forms of freedom throughout the course of the story. In other fictions, James uses architectural images to define his characters' inner states, but here he does it so masterfully that the reader can follow Isabel's progress toward and away from freedom simply by looking at her relationship with the various rooms and residences she occupies.

When we first encounter Isabel, she is in the gloomiest room of the family home, a place of "mysterious melancholy" known as the office. We are told that "she might have had the whole house to choose from, and the room she had selected was the most depressed of its scenes," in part because its main door is a "silent, motionless portal ... secured by bolts which a particularly slender little girl found it impossible to slide."69 Here she is found by her Aunt Lydia, who takes Isabel away from this gloomy cell and installs her at Gardencourt, the Touchett estate in England and Isabel's departure point for what promises to be a life of well-appointed freedom.

Fittingly, our first view of Gardencourt is one that suggests expansiveness. Rather than see a gloomy interior, or any interior at all, we are shown a group of people at tea on the lawn. But this lawn is unlike others, for "the wide carpet of turf that covered the level hill-top seemed but the extension of a luxurious interior. The great still oaks and beeches flung down a shade as dense as that of velvet curtains; and the place was furnished, like a room, with cushioned seats, with rich-coloured rugs, with the books and papers that lay upon the grass."70 The atmosphere at Gardencourt seems so conducive to freedom that the very walls have disappeared. The presiding genius at Gardencourt is Isabel's uncle, Daniel Touchett, and even his teacup seems suggestive of possibilities: it is "an unusually large cup, of a different pattern from the rest of the set and painted in brilliant colours."71

Almost at once, Isabel receives a proposal of marriage from the Touchetts' neighbor, Lord Warburton, and the paradoxical nature of freedom becomes apparent, for while she

views marriage to Warburton as a form of pleasant confinement, he sees it quite otherwise. She tells him that she
could never be happy by separating herself "'from life. From
the usual chances and dangers, from what most people know
and suffer.'" Warburton expostulates, saying, "'I don't offer
you any exoneration from life or from any chances or dangers
whatever. I wish I could; depend upon it I would! For what
do you take me, pray? Heaven help me, I'm not the Emperor
of China! All I offer you is the chance of taking the common
lot in a comfortable way.'"72 But at this early stage in her
career, too much comfort seems as threatening to Isabel as
too much discomfort. Incidentally, while both Gardencourt
and Lockleigh (Warburton's residence) are referred to as
houses, the latter is surrounded by a "broad, still moat" and
it reminds Isabel of a "castle in a legend."73 Though it may
have a certain Old World charm, Lockleigh is a little too secure for our eager young democrat.

Importuned not only by Warburton but also by Caspar
Goodwood, an American suitor, Isabel leaves England in
search of broader vistas to the south. She will meet an unexpected fate in Italy, but for the moment, all seems well:
"The charm of the Mediterranean coast only deepened for our
heroine on acquaintance, for it was the threshold of Italy, the
gate of admirations. Italy, as yet imperfectly seen and felt,
stretched before her as a land of promise, a land in which a
love of the beautiful might be comforted by endless knowledge."74

This general splendor notwithstanding, the particular
reality of life in Italy will be rather different for Isabel. An
ominous note is sounded in the description of the house of
Gilbert Osmond, who will be Isabel's husband:

> The house had a front upon a little grassy, empty,
> rural piazza which occupied a part of the hill-top;
> and this front, pierced with a few windows in ir-
> regular relations and furnished with a stone bench
> lengthily adjusted to the base of the structure and
> useful as a lounging-place to one or two persons
> wearing more or less of that air of undervalued
> merit which in Italy, for some reason or other,
> always gracefully invests anyone who confidently
> assumes a perfectly passive attitude--this antique,
> solid, weather-worn, yet imposing front had a
> somewhat incommunicative character. It was the
> mask, not the face of the house. It had heavy lids,

> but no eyes; the house in reality looked another
> way--looked off behind, into splendid openness and
> the range of the afternoon light. 75

The description of the house having "heavy lids, but
no eyes" seems metaphorical, but in fact it is a very accurate characterization of the Villa Castellani, now called the
Villa Mercede, an old house on the hill of Bellosguardo just
outside Florence. James's friends Francis and Lizzie Boott,
a father and daughter who suggested the characters of Gilbert
and Pansy Osmond to James, lived there, as did James himself for a time. I recall my surprise on seeing the Villa
Mercede for the first time some years ago and noting that
its heavily barred windows with their thick stucco overhangs
were indeed suggestive of a coarse, blind face. Passing
through the principal entrance, one finds oneself in "a wide,
high court, where a clear shadow rested below and a pair of
light-arched galleries, facing each other above, caught the
upper sunshine upon their slim columns and the flowering
plants in which they were dressed." If there is a certain
delicacy in this description, it is the delicacy of mesh, not
gossamer. The first time Isabel sees this courtyard, she
thinks, "There was something grave and strong in the place;
it looked somehow as if, once you were in, you would need
an act of energy to get out."76

More architectural imagery, combined this time with
images of flight, is used in the pages that follow to contrast
the generous character of Isabel with the mean one of Osmond.
Several weeks after their first meeing, these two and their
friends are in Rome, where Isabel visits and is filled with
awe by the magnificence of St. Peter's Cathedral.

> She had not been one of the superior tourists who
> are "disappointed" in Saint Peter's and find it
> smaller than its fame; the first time she passed
> beneath the huge leathern curtain that strains and
> bangs at the entrance, the first time she found her-
> self beneath the far-arching dome and saw the light
> drizzle down through the air thickened with incense
> and with the reflections of marble and gilt, of mo-
> saic and bronze, her conception of greatness rose
> and dizzily rose. After this it never lacked space
> to soar. 77

But Osmond's views of this architectural wonder are quite
different.

"What's your opinion of Saint Peter's?" Mr.
Osmond was meanwhile enquiring of our young lady.
"It's very large and very bright," she contented
herself with replying.
"It's too large; it makes one feel like an atom."
"Isn't that the right way to feel in the greatest
of human temples?" she asked with rather a liking
for her phrase.
"I suppose it's the right way to feel everywhere,
when one is nobody. But I like it in a church as
little as anywhere else."
"You ought indeed to be a Pope!" Isabel ex-
claimed, remembering something he had referred
to in Florence.
"Ah, I should have enjoyed that!" said Gilbert
Osmond. [78]

Whether or not one detects a shudder of James's New England sensibility behind the papal reference, the point is made
convincingly that Osmond is power-hungry precisely because
he thinks of himself as small and powerless.

One way for him to exercise power is by cutting Isabel down to size. When she tells her cousin Ralph that she
and Osmond are engaged, Ralph finds it hard to believe that
she would terminate her rise so abruptly, and for such a man.

"I think I've hardly got over my surprise," he
went on at last. "You were the last person I ex-
pected to see caught."
"I don't know why you call it caught."
"Because you're going to be put into a cage."
"If I like my cage, that needn't trouble you."[79]

But Ralph is not convinced by Isabel's bold talk.

"I had treated myself to a charming vision of
your future," Ralph observed without answering
this; "I had amused myself with planning out a high
destiny for you. There was to be nothing of this
sort in it. You were not to come down so easily
or so soon."
"Come down, you say?"
"Well, that renders my sense of what has happened to you. You seemed to me to be soaring far
up in the blue--to be, sailing in the bright light,
over the heads of men. Suddenly some one tosses

up a faded rosebud--a missile that should never
have reached you--and straight you drop to the
ground. It hurts me," said Ralph audaciously,
"hurts me as if I had fallen myself!"

The look of pain and bewilderment deepened in
his companion's face. "I don't understand you in
the least," she repeated. "You say you amused
yourself with a project for my career--I don't
understand that. Don't amuse yourself too much,
or I shall think you're doing it at my expense."

Ralph shook his head. "I'm not afraid of your
not believing that I've had great ideas for you."

"What do you mean by my soaring and sailing?"
she pursued. "I've never moved on a higher plane
than I'm moving on now. There's nothing higher
for a girl than to marry a--a person she likes,"
said poor Isabel, wandering into the didactic.

"It's your liking the person we speak of that I
venture to criticise, my dear cousin. I should
have said that the man for you would have been a
more active, larger, freer sort of nature." Ralph
hesitated, then added: "I can't get over the sense
that Osmond is somehow--well, small." He had uttered the last word with no great assurance; he was
afraid she would flash out again. But to his surprise she was quiet; she had the air of considering.

"Small?" She made it sound immense.

"I think he's narrow, selfish. He takes himself
so seriously!"[80]

Ralph is right, of course. Osmond wastes no time
in caging and domesticating Isabel. As if to indicate the hopelessness of her captivity, James moves the action from deceptive prison that is Osmond's house in Florence to the obvious prison of the Palazzo Roccanera (literally "black for-
tress"), Osmond's Roman residence. This edifice is care-
fully scrutinized by one Ned Rosier, a suitor for the hand
of Pansy Osmond. But her father keeps Pansy as closely
caged as her stepmother.

The object of Mr. Rosier's well-regulated affection
dwelt in a high house in the very heart of Rome;
a dark and massive structure overlooking a sunny
piazzetta in the neighbourhood of the Farnese Palace.
In a palace, too, little Pansy lived--a palace by
Roman measure, but a dungeon to poor Rosier's
apprehensive mind. It seemed to him of evil omen

that the young lady he wished to marry, and whose
fastidious father he doubted of his ability to concil-
iate, should be immured in a kind of domestic for-
tress, a pile which bore a stern old Roman name,
which smelt of crime and craft and violence.... In
a less preoccupied frame of mind he could have done
justice to the Palazzo Roccanera; he could have entered into the sentiment of Mrs. Osmond, who had
once told him that on settling themselves in Rome
she and her husband had chosen this habitation for
the love of local colour. It had local colour enough,
and though he knew less about architecture than about
Limoges enamels he could see that the proportions
of the windows and even the details of the cornice
had quite the grand air. But Rosier was haunted
by the conviction that at picturesque periods young
girls had been shut up there to keep them from
their true loves, and then, under the threat of being thrown into convents, had been forced into unholy marriages. [81]

Pansy is of course thrown into a convent following the
socially ambitious Osmond's bungled attempt to marry her
off to Lord Warburton. Though he is an aristocrat, Warburton is opposed to the idea of arranged marriages, and when
he realizes that Pansy does not love him, he withdraws his
suit, making Pansy the second woman in the novel to escape
confinement in Warburton's castle. [82] But the convent represents a fate that is hardly preferable. Osmond puts Pansy
there partly to get her away from the influence of those such
as Isabel and his own sister, the Countess Gemini, who might
encourage Pansy to have independent thoughts, and partly to
chasten her, to make her realize that she will be punished
if she does not obey him in matters of marriage as in all
others. The subtly threatening language that Osmond uses to
describe his reasons for confining Pansy is made doubly odi-
ous by his hypocrisy:

"Pansy's a little dusty, a little dishevelled; she has
knocked about too much. This bustling, pushy rab-
ble that calls itself society--one should take her
out of it occasionally. Convents are very quiet,
very convenient, very salutary. I like to think of
her there, in the old garden, under the arcade,
among those tranquil, virtuous women. Many of
them are gentlewomen born; several of them are
noble. She will have her books and her drawing,

> she will have her piano. I've made the most lib-
> eral arrangements. There is to be nothing ascetic;
> there's just to be a certain little sense of seques-
> tration. "[83]

But the implications of Pansy's confinement are much
more sinister than this. Her stay in the convent is, in fact,
a parody of the monastic retreat that Osmond pretends it is.
Isabel realizes this when she goes to visit Pansy:

> Isabel had been at this institution before; she had
> come with Pansy to see the sisters. She knew
> they were good women, and she saw that the large
> rooms were clean and cheerful and that the well-
> used garden had sun for winter and shade for spring.
> But she disliked the place, which affronted and al-
> most frightened her; not for the world would she
> have spent a night there. It produced to-day more
> than before the impression of a well-appointed
> prison; for it was not possible to pretend that Pansy
> was free to leave it. [84]

If, in addition to these impressions, Isabel finds the
convent " 'quiet,' " as Osmond calls it, at least she knows by
now that horror is not always noisy. In fact, the word
"quiet," along with its various synonyms, occurs a number
of times in the text, and it is a measure of Isabel's developing consciousness that she learns to tell the difference between the religious quietism that is associated with monism
and the deceptive kind that makes an aggressive intent. Isabel finds the Misses Molyneux, Warburton's sisters, " 'quiet
and reasonable and satisfied,' " as she tells Ralph Touchett,
and vows, " 'I mean to try and imitate them.' "[85] The elder
of the two sisters has a "smooth, nun-like forehead" and
wears a "large silver cross suspended from her neck"; she
is Isabel's favorite because there is "such a world of hered-
itary quiet in her."[86] Ralph himself is variously described
as "indifferent" and "passive," in his own words and in those
of Isabel's friend Henrietta Stackpole.[87] Yet Ralph is an
"apostle of freedom."[88]

Between such characters as these and the deceptively
quiet ones who plot against Isabel there is Pansy, who strikes
the reader as delightfully fresh and modest until it is revealed
that she has no freedom of choice and has been raised as a
robot. On the eve of entering the convent, when Pansy says,
" 'I shall be very quiet,' " she is simply telling us what she has
done all along. [89]

Osmond is the most dangerous and therefore the most important of the deceptively passive characters, of course, but he is nearly matched by his accomplice, Madame Merle, whose

> old habit had been to live by enthusiasm, to fall in love with suddenly-perceived possibilities, with the idea of some new adventure. As a younger person she had been used to proceed from one little exaltation to the other: there were scarcely any dull places between. But Madame Merle had suppressed enthusiasm; she fell in love now-a-days with nothing; she lived entirely by reason and by wisdom. There were hours when Isabel would have given anything for lessons in this art; if her brilliant friend had been near she would have made an appeal to her. She had become aware more than before of the advantage of being like that--of having made one's self a firm surface, a sort of corselet of silver.... Madame Merle's conduct, to her perception, always bore the stamp of good taste, was always "quiet."[90]

One might think Isabel glad to be rid of those who have betrayed her into an unhappy marriage, which is why her return to Osmond at the end of the novel is one of the most baffling and frustrating conclusions in literature. I believe her return is best understood in terms of a particular motif that runs throughout The Portrait of a Lady. This is the chain of promises that Isabel makes and breaks and, most interesting of all, the ones that she avoids altogether. In Chapter 16, for instance, she not only rejects Caspar Goodwood's offer of marriage (just as she has recently rejected Lord Warburton's) but also she refuses to guarantee that she will be more receptive to him in the future. "'Ah, remember,'" she says, "'I promise nothing--absolutely nothing!'"[91] Caspar is easily the most importunate of her suitors (who also include not only Warburton and Gilbert Osmond but even, in his way, Ralph Touchett) and he represents best the trap that Isabel must avoid if she is to remain entirely independent: the trap of the unbreakable promise, particularly the promise of marriage. Thus, Isabel is no less surprised than Caspar when, in a relatively brief time, she agrees to marry Gilbert Osmond. It is the first really solemn commitment that she makes, and she does so in the face of odds that can only be described as discouraging, for there is not a single marriage in the novel that inspires confidence. Paradoxically, Isabel

thinks that she is most free just when she capitulates to the
tyranny of her whimsical nature.

By Chapter 48, Isabel has, she thinks, learned her
lesson. When her friend Henrietta Stackpole asks her to
leave Osmond, Isabel says, "'I shall never make another
promise. I made such a solemn one four years ago [she
refers to her marriage vow], and I've succeeded so ill in
keeping it.'"[92] And within a few chapters, she seems to
have regained her old independence. When Osmond forbids
her to go to the bedside of Ralph, who is dying in England,
she goes anyway, stopping only long enough to say goodbye
to Pansy, who is in the convent that reminds Isabel of a
prison. And it is in the convent that she makes--somewhat
against her will--her second solemn promise, which is to
rescue Pansy after she comes back from England. This is
another promise that, it seems, she will "succeed ill in keeping," for she has the opportunity to run away with Caspar
Goodwood, who conveniently turns up to offer, if not the
chance for true love, at least protection and support for a
runaway wife. But this time she resists the tyranny of the
whim. When Caspar takes Isabel in his arms, the reader
is told that "his kiss was like white lightning, a flash that
spread, and spread again, and stayed.... But when darkness
returned she was free."[93]

With Ralph Touchett dead and Lord Warburton perman-
ently discouraged, the final battle for Isabel's hand is waged
by a black magician against a white one, Osmond versus
Caspar Goodwood. In his brilliant and exhaustive study of
connections between The Portrait of a Lady and popular literature, William Veeder details Osmond's literary pedigree of
evil, only part of which is reported here:

> Seeking a name for his villain in The Castle Spec-
> tre, Monk Lewis may well have gone back (con-
> sciously or unconsciously) to a bloody and exotic
> drama of the British theatrical past, Osmond, the
> Great Turk. For certain we find in Lewis' peren-
> ially popular play several details so similar to de-
> tails in The Portrait that we should examine them.
> The Castle Spectre contains, for example, a "knave"
> named Gilbert (I i). His master is "Osmond ...
> the very antidote of mirth" (I i). In his pursuit
> of the heroine, Osmond is thwarted both by "the
> Portrait of a Lady" (III iii) which swings back to
> reveal a convenient passage-way and by the lady

of that portrait, who comes back (as a ghost) to
save her daughter from incarceration by Osmond.
Before the Beset Heroine escapes, however, she
endures a dark night "allowed you to reflect upon
your situation" (III iii). (I cannot resist adding
that the heroine's duenna exclaims, "oh gemini"
[III iii].) After The Castle Spectre we find the
romantics christening characters "Osman" and
"Osmyn" and the name "Ormond" appearing in both
Maria Edgeworth and Charles Brockden Brown. In
America the name Osmond itself appears as early
as 1804, in Alicia La Fanu's Lucy Osmond. This
story of betrayed heroines, inadequate guardians,
and sudden fortunes is then followed in the 1830s
by a terrifically successful play, Lucy Leslie, the
Cottager's Daughter; or, The Maid, the Mother and
the Maniac. Here "poor Lucy is shot down by her
betrayer, Osmond, when he learns she is not, as
he has been led to believe, the heiress to fifty
thousand pounds. "94

These Osmonds, Osmans, and Osmyns are appropriate an-
cestors for one who is thoroughly evil and who wants to control Isabel completely. As for Goodwood, the power with
which he threatens Isabel is as insidious as, if less sinister
than, the cold tyranny of Osmond. The point is that Isabel
does not want to be anyone's Trilby. She breaks the spell
of the black magician when she goes to London in defiance
of his command; she breaks the spell of the white magician
when she resists the transforming power of his kiss.

All this talk of magic aside, there is nothing supernatural about the strength of mind used by Isabel to thwart
Osmond and Goodwood. It develops slowly and remains uncertain and fallible, like any human creation. Halfway through
the novel, Isabel has done little more than accumulate the
experience that will serve as grist for her meditative mill
(as Maggie Tulliver in The Mill on the Floss could not, due
to her early death). One particular incident starts a chain
of events that will culminate in Isabel's self-liberation, however, an incident that is trivial in itself yet that is invested
with the utmost significance by Isabel's developing consciousness. The incident occurs when Isabel returns home unex-
pectedly to find Gilbert Osmond and Madame Merle together
in the drawing-room of the Palazzo Roccanera.

Madame Merle was standing on the rug, a little way

> from the fire; Osmond was in a deep chair, lean-
> ing back and looking at her.  Her head was erect,
> as usual, but her eyes were bent on his.  What
> struck Isabel first was that he was sitting while
> Madame Merle stood; there was an anomaly in this
> that arrested her.  Then she perceived that they
> had arrived at a desultory pause in their exchange
> of ideas and were musing face to face, with the
> freedom of old friends who sometimes exchange
> ideas without uttering them.  There was nothing
> to shock in this; they were old friends in fact.
> But the thing made an image, lasting only a mo-
> ment, like a sudden flicker of light. [95]

This flicker of light illuminates little; though it is odd for a
gentleman to seat himself before a lady who is not his wife,
and though there are even subtler reverberations that Isabel
cannot apprehend rationally, still, there is nothing about this
scene to cause immediate alarm.  There is in the physical
attitudes of Osmond and Merle something of significance, however, and Isabel will revert to the scene in the pages that
follow.

Chapter 42 of The Portrait of a Lady is taken up entirely with one of the most celebrated scenes in American
fiction, Isabel's night-long vigil.  Osmond bids her to help
him marry off Pansy to Warburton, and "for a long time,
far into the night and still further, she sat in the still drawing-room, given up to her meditation.  A servant came in to
attend to the fire, and she bade him bring fresh candles and
then go to bed.  Osmond had told her to think of what he had
said; and she did so indeed, and of many other things."  Impressions come and go in Isabel's mind over the course of
the next ten pages, just as scenes, snatches of conversation,
and memories of all sorts rise and fall in the minds of those
who practice meditation in the traditional sense. [96]  And as
in traditional meditation, much of what occurs to Isabel is
troubling:

> Her soul was haunted with terrors which crowded
> to the foreground of thought as quickly as a place
> was made for them.  What had suddenly set them
> into livelier motion she hardly knew, unless it were
> the strange impression she had received in the
> afternoon of her husband's being in more direct
> communication with Madame Merle than she sus-
> pected.  That impression came back to her from

time to time, and now she wondered it had never
come before.

Eventually, Isabel leaves off thinking about the Osmond-
Merle connection and turns to her own relationship with her
husband and her "failing faith" in that relationship.

> It had come gradually--it was not till the first
> year of their life together, so admirably intimate
> at first, had closed that she had taken the alarm.
> Then the shadows had begun to gather; it was as
> if Osmond deliberately, almost malignantly, had put
> the lights out one by one. The dusk at first was
> vague and thin, and she could still see her way in
> it. But it steadily deepened, and if now and again
> it had occasionally lifted there were certain corners
> of her prospect that were impenetrably black.
> These shadows were not an emanation from her
> own mind: she was very sure of that; she had done
> her best to be just and temperate, to see only the
> truth. They were a part, they were a kind of cre-
> ation and consequence, of her husband's very pres-
> ence.

The idea of Osmond turning out the lights one by one recalls
the image that James uses in the preface to The Awkward
Age, a kind of mirror of the above in which lights are turned
on one by one in order to illuminate fully, not benight. A
dim consciousness is precisely what Osmond wants for Isabel,
of course; "he had said to her one day that she had too many
ideas and that she must get rid of them.... He had really
meant it--he would have liked her to have nothing of her own
but her pretty appearance." In other words, Osmond would
make of Isabel what he has made of Pansy, a realization that
explains Isabel's identification with Pansy and her resolve to
save her at the novel's end.

Architectural imagery recurs as Isabel comes to understand Osmond's subtle tyranny:

> When, as the months had elapsed, she had followed
> him further and he had led her into the mansion
> of his own habitation, then, then she had seen where
> she really was.
> She could live it over again, the incredulous ter-
> ror with which she had taken the measure of her
> dwelling. Between those four walls she had lived

> ever since; they were to surround her for the rest
> of her life. It was the house of darkness, the
> house of dumbness, the house of suffocation. Os-
> mond's beautiful mind gave it neither light nor air;
> Osmond's beautiful mind indeed seemed to peep down
> from a small high window and mock at her.

There are many such torturous moments in the course of
Isabel's vigil, but by the time morning comes, she has
achieved a clarity of mind that will prove essential to her
right conduct in the future.

> For herself, she lingered in the soundless saloon
> long after the fire had gone out. There was no dan-
> ger of her feeling the cold; she was in a fever. She
> heard the small hours strike, and then the great
> ones, but her vigil took no heed of time. Her
> mind, assailed by visions, was in a state of extra-
> ordinary activity, and her visions might as well
> come to her there, where she sat up to meet them,
> as on her pillow, to make a mockery of rest. As
> I have said, she believed she was not defiant, and
> what could be a better proof of it than that she
> should linger there half the night, trying to persuade
> herself that there was no reason why Pansy shouldn't
> be married as you would put a letter in the post-
> office? When the clock struck four she got up; she
> was going to bed at last, for the lamp had long
> since gone out and the candles burned down to their
> sockets. But even then she stopped again in the
> middle of the room and stood there gazing at a re-
> membered vision--that of her husband and Madame
> Merle unconsciously and familiarly associated. 97

Meditation can only supply ideas, not verify them,
and Isabel is not certain of the exact nature of the relationship between her husband and his friend until the Countess
Gemini tells her outright that Madame Merle was Osmond's
mistress for some years and that Pansy is her daughter, not
the daughter of Osmond's deceased first wife. 98 And Isabel
must suffer much in the hundred pages or so to come as well
as "after" the novel's end, no doubt. But at least she begins
to suspect during her vigil that she has been conspired against
by Merle and Osmond and, more important, she realizes the
depth of Osmond's iniquity. What she discerns at this point
in the novel makes it possible for her to be decisive at the
end when she spurns Goodwood's offer and returns to Rome

to free Pansy and to emulate the Zen shoemaker who, upon
attaining enlightenment, went back to making shoes.

★

But how tenuous this seems, how effete. No wonder there
is often an ugly quality to the sneerings of James's detractors, as though there is more at stake than a mere denial of
affinities. To those who do not like him, it is not always a
matter of James's being out of line philosophically or aes-
thetically. It is more a question of his being insufficiently
manly or American or both. To his enemies, James comes
off as a sissy's sissy, a cosmopolitan momma's boy, the
ultimate international wimp. Teddy Roosevelt called James
"a miserable little snob" and wrote that James's stories
"make one blush to think that he was once an American";
this was in 1894, when James, who did not become a British
citizen until 1915, was as much an American as Roosevelt
was. [99] (In turn, James described Roosevelt as "a dangerous
and ominous jingo" and, more characteristically, "the mere
monstrous embodiment of unprecedented and resounding
noise."[100]) Even discerning critics of James--Sallie Sears
and Quentin Anderson are two who are sometimes cited--are
capable of concluding that his imagination is negative and es-
capist in nature. [101]

But despite Roosevelt's effort to isolate James and
represent him as a neurotic exception, it is clear that his
seemingly passive and retiring heroes and heroines belong
not only to a worldwide literary, philosophical, and religious
tradition of monism and quietism from the Bible to Borges
but also to a specifically American one that goes from Hawthorne through Heller and beyond. One critic who sees this
with particular clarity, though probably he would be surprised
to have his viewpoint associated with my own argument, is
Daniel Schneider, author of The Crystal Cage: Adventures
of the Imagination in the Fiction of Henry James. [102] There
is little in his book that is entirely new, yet Schneider ex-
tends what is known about James through every level of his
work and gives us a more comprehensive understanding of
James's imagination than any other critic of his to date. One
might take the matter of imagery, for example: Charles R.
Anderson, Robert Gale, and Philip M. Weinstein have cata-
loged and commented on James's use of locks, walls, cages,
and so on to suggest entrapment, but Schneider shows the
connection between these images and such common verbs as
square, fix, hold, take hold of, handle, check, grasp, and

clutch. 103  This is to say that the reader comes away with
a heightened sense of just how thoroughly and subtly James
has filled his imaginary world with snares--one steps back
from a frightening image only to find oneself caught in a trap
made of very fatal, very ordinary words.

To succeed in James's world is to be free rather than
happy, and freedom comes through detachment, a word
Schneider uses often.   But detachment is not denial in James,
no matter what his detractors may say.   Rather, it is a
means by which a character may, through self-discipline,
rise above a selfish, strife-torn, and enslaving world.   It
should not be surprising that there is such strong interest
in James's fiction in Japan, for a Buddhist would say that
James's ideal characters are freed from life and thus freed
for life.   At the ends of their stories, such characters as
Christopher Newman, Isabel Archer, and Lambert Strether
are, after long struggles, free from the grossness of human
passions and ambitions, which means they can take up their
obligations once more in a spirit that is at once detached and
compassionate.   According to orthodox Western thinking,
they are losers, for dualistic Western thought predicates the
acquisition, the management, the conquering of the Other lest
it acquire, manage, and conquer us.

This way of thinking is all right for Teddy Roosevelt,
but what James seems to have in mind is rather different.
In his Confessions, Augustine wrote:  "I was unhappy and so
is every soul unhappy which is tied to its love for mortal
things; when it loses them, it is torn to pieces, and it is
then that it comes to realize the unhappiness which was there
even before it lost them."   James's books are filled with col-
lectors of "mortal things."   Gilbert Osmond, clearly not a
happy man, is one such collector.   In contrast, Isabel Archer
is hardly happy, but then that is not the Jamesian goal; freedom is.

In one of the most celebrated epiphanies in modern
literature, Isabel comes to realize the truth about her un-
fortunate marriage to Osmond in the course of the meditation,
discussed above, that parallels the actual practice of adepts.
That is, rather than following a sequential thought pattern and
working things out logically, she sits quietly before a fire
and allows her mind to come and go from the problem until
the truth manifests itself intuitively.   Free from illusion, she
returns to the phenomenal world and acts in a way that is
baffling to many readers.   At the novel's end, she rejects

the devoted Caspar Goodwood, as she must to retain her freedom. Moreover, she returns to Osmond, which is to say she
returns to what she knows. Knowing it, she is free from it;
she might have entered into an attachment with Caspar Goodwood, but she is truly free for the first time in her life and
unwilling to trade her freedom for happiness that may be only
transitory.

Seen this way, James's entire career can be understood as a meditation on detachment, its drawbacks as well
as its merits. There are genuine cris de coeur, such as
"The Beast in the Jungle," a kind of literary Gethsemane in
which James laments a life unlived. There are magnificently
moving depictions of tragic entrapment, such as The Wings
of the Dove. And then there are such works as The Portrait
of a Lady, in which liberty is acheived, though at a price.
Schneider's chapter "The Divided Self" describes the soul's
tenuous journey as detailed by James; in that chapter and
throughout his book Schneider makes it clear that James is
a novelist of process rather than ideas. As they err and
triumph, James's characters are trying simply to Get It
Right. That is their business and the artist's as well, and
it does not serve to moralize or expostulate, to tell others
how their lives should be lived. Schneider quotes James's
advice to Violet Paget: "Morality is hot--but art is icy."
The world is hot with passion and strife, and even to struggle
against the world is to burn in its flames. Coolness and detachment are the only means of survival.

There is nothing restrictively Eastern or Buddhist
about James's thought, of course, and certainly no case is
made here for influence. Schneider is in fact, careful to
bring in such figures as Plato (whose distinction between
false appearance and true reality is useful to an understanding of James) and Meister Eckhart (who placed detachment
above love in his catalogue of virtues) in order to put James
in the Western intellectual tradition. The point is that James
participates in the great dialogue of minds from all lands and
all ages as distinguished from the narrow war-room chatter
of Teddy Roosevelt and his epigones. The subject of the
dialogue is freedom, not conquest. "'The ladies will save
us,'" says Daniel Touchett, Ralph's father, in the first chapter of The Portrait of a Lady. [104] Perhaps they will not;
perhaps they will not even save themselves. But in James
they are at least free to try.

5

## HEART OF DARKNESS

> "Live rightly, die, die."

Money is a perennial favorite among literary themes because it is both basic and ambiguous.  Everyone wants it, yet money alone does not satisfy; as Freud says, the love of money is an adult passion, and we experience pleasure only when our infantile desires are gratified.

The pursuit of money is always problematic: " 'Money's a horrid thing to follow, but a charming thing to meet,' " says Isabel Archer. [1]  Certainly, money is important in The Portrait of a Lady.  It plays a central, if less obvious, role in The Mill on the Floss (the ruining of Maggie Tulliver's father by Lawyer Wakem is fatal to the happiness of her family). And money is almost a medium, like air or water, in the Wall Street world of "Bartleby the Scrivener."  But nowhere are the stakes as high as they are in Heart of Darkness, where Money becomes Empire and the desire to be wealthy becomes the categorical need to control others.

In the phenomenal world, the quest for Empire is the greatest of goals, the starkest of dualities.  As such, it can never be described honestly and is therefore discussed in religious, philanthropic, patriotic, even philosophic terms.  One wants to save heathens, succor the poor and hungry, extend the benefits of democracy to savages, bring "order out of chaos," as Teddy Roosevelt said in describing the American mission in the Philippines.  At heart, the desire for Empire is different only in degree, not in kind, from Osmond's desire for dominion over Isabel Archer and her fortune.  It is the same greedy visage, heavy with paint, yet multiplied a thousandfold.  The horror we feel on reading The Portrait stems from our empathy with Isabel, our feeling that if it could happen to her, with all her attributes and good inten-

110

tions, then It Could Happen To Us.  The horror we feel on
reading Heart of Darkness stems from our sense of complicity, our understanding that It Is Happening To Us Right Now.

The Belgian Congo seems remote; it isn't even called
the Congo anymore.  Yet Conrad not only suggests but also
emphasizes the connection between the Congo and our world
by means of his story frame.  The main action takes place
in the Congo, but the story is told by a narrator who has
heard it first on the deck of the Nellie, a yawl that cruises
the Thames.  A conflation of sentences from the second and
the last paragraphs of Heart of Darkness makes evident the
connection between the "civilized" world and the other:  "The
sea-reach of the Thames stretched before us like the beginning of an interminable waterway ... and the tranquil waterway leading to the uttermost ends of the earth flowed sombre
under an overcast sky--seemed to lead into the heart of an
immense darkness."2  And before he begins to detail the
Congo and its inhabitants, Conrad expands on the themes of
commerce and conquest in a kind of ironic eulogy of the
Thames.

> It had known and served all the men of whom the
> nation is proud, from Sir Francis Drake to Sir
> John Franklin, knights all, titled and untitled--the
> great knights-errant of the sea.  It had borne all
> the ships whose names are like jewels flashing in
> the night of time, from the Golden Hind returning
> with her round flanks full of treasure, to be visited
> by the Queen's Highness and thus pass out of the
> gigantic tale, to the Erebus and Terror, bound on
> other conquests--and that never returned.  It had
> known the ships and the men.  They had sailed
> from Deptford, from Greenwich, from Erith--the
> adventurers and the settlers; kings' ships and the
> ships of men on 'Change; captains, admirals, the
> dark "interlopers" of the Eastern trade, and the
> commissioned "generals" of East India fleets.
> Hunters for gold or pursuers of fame, they had
> all gone out on that stream, bearing the sword,
> and often the torch, messengers of the might within
> the land, bearers of a spark from the sacred fire.
> What greatness had not floated on the ebb of that
> river into the mystery of an unknown earth! ...
> The dreams of men, the seed of commonwealths,
> the germs of empires. 3

The atmosphere in the story proper, in the Congo, is hellish. Aboard the Nellie, however, in the frame that surrounds Marlow's narrative, the mood bespeaks an Oriental quietude. The first mention of Marlow, who tells the story that the narrator passes along to us, has him sitting "cross-legged ... with his arms dropped, the palms of hands outwards, [he] resembled an idol." A few pages later, it is said that, "with his legs folded before him, he had the pose of a Buddha preaching in European clothes and without a lotus-flower." And in the book's last paragraph he is described as sitting "in the pose of a meditating Buddha."[4]

Marlow's quasi-religious peacefulness is not wasted on his audience aboard the Nellie, four friends--the Director, the Accountant, the Lawyer, and the narrator himself--who are called "meditative."[5] And when the Buddha-like Marlow gets around to speaking to them, he does in fact describe a religion rich in resources and organization, the religion of Empire. Yet it is the religion of darkness, not light. "'It was just robbery with violence,'" says Marlow, "'aggravated murder on a great scale, and men going at it blind--as is very proper for those who tackle a darkness.'" What makes this a religion instead of merely instinctive rapaciousness is the idea behind it, the European imperialist idea of bringing civilization in return for extracting wealth. According to Marlow, this idea is "'something you can set up, and bow down before, and offer a sacrifice to....'"[6]

If Marlow is peaceful and meditative aboard the Nellie, it is not because these qualities are inherent to his character. His calm is that of one who has passed through the fire, who has felt the heat of the world and is now regarding it from a distance, with cool tranquility. Knowing what kind of men are drawn to the heart of darkness, the company doctor who examines Marlow before his departure advises him to "'"avoid irritation ... keep calm."'"[7] This advice is especially sound for one who is about to descend to a Dantesque world lorded over by "'a flabby, pretending, weak-eyed devil,'" a place that recalls "'the gloomy circle of some Inferno,'" where the Company's chief accountant appears as a "'miracle,'" where the manager of the Central Station is a "'papier-mâché Mephistopheles,'" where a gang of ivory hunters is "'a lot of faithless pilgrims.'"[8]

This setting is as crowded, noisy, and confusing as that of a medieval morality play. At its center is Kurtz, already chief of the Inner Station (the soul?). It is predicted

that before long he will be the ruler of a much larger domain, one that is not specified and is therefore potentially
limitless. 9   All mere hints about his being a, if not the,
devil cease when Marlow actually meets Kurtz:   " 'The thing
was to know to what he belonged to, how many powers of
darkness claimed him for their own,' " says Marlow, although
he is sure that " 'he had taken a high seat amongst the devils
of the land--I mean literally. ' "10   An Antichrist, a false
messiah, Kurtz preaches love to his disciples. 11   Yet he
presides " 'at certain midnight dances ending with unspeakable
rites' " and he puts the heads of his enemies on stakes that
face his house. 12

As with Marlow, the Kurtz we meet is not the same
as the one who went to the Congo in the first place.   But
whereas the darkness has chastened Marlow, it has corrupted
Kurtz.   Though the stimulus of the wild is the same in both
cases, the reaction to it differs.   Attempting to define what
happened to Kurtz, critic Jeffrey Meyers quotes from
Walden in order to show the effect of the wilderness on the
ordinarily pacific Thoreau:

> I caught a glimpse of a woodchuck stealing across
> my path, and felt a strange thrill of savage delight,
> and I was strongly tempted to seize and devour him
> raw; not that I was hungry then, except for that
> wilderness which he represented.... I found my-
> self ranging the woods, like a half-starved hound,
> with a strange abandonment, seeking some kind of
> venison which I might devour, and no morsel could
> have been too savage for me. 13

Such an act, especially as it is unrelated to hunger, is an
exercise of the will to power, a God-like desire.   And in
fact Kurtz's story is to some extent the story of Faust, who
acquired God's power but not His wisdom.   In addition to his
regular duties for the Company, Kurtz has been asked to
write a report for the International Society for the Suppres-
sion of Savage Customs.   The report begins with the assertion
that civilized people " ' "must necessarily appear to [savages]
in the nature of supernatural beings--we approach them with
the might as of a deity. " ' "14   The problem is that he comes
to believe his own report and begins to play God--the ultimate temptation, the absolute polar opposite of the calm and
avoidance of irritation that the company doctor recommends.
He creates his own hell; worse, he imposes it on others.
As Thomas Merton says of the Renaissance explorers, "in

subjugating primitive worlds they only imposed on them, with the force of cannons, their own confusion and alienation. "[15]

Insofar as life imitates art, our own time has offered us numerous leaders of the Kurtz type: Hitler, say, or, at about the time that I began this study, the Reverend Jim Jones of Guyana. [16] Like Kurtz, Jones approached his congregation "'"with the might as of a deity."'" He saw himself as the embodiment of holiness, telling his followers that he was "the reincarnation not only of Father Divine and Christ, but of Buddha and Stalin and God as well. "[17] Also like Kurtz, Jones encouraged the adulation of the faithful. This is a virtual proof of falsity in itself; the Gnostic Jesus and even the Jesus of the New Testament discouraged worship, and it is traditional today as in the past for Hindu and Buddhist sages to send overly ardent disciples to other masters in order to prevent the development of cults of personality. By way of contrast, from time to time Jones would throw the Bible to the floor, shouting: "'Too many people are looking at this and not at me.'"[18]

A figure like Kurtz or Jones fills the screen; they wanted to be larger than life, and to some extent they were. Yet the objects of real bafflement are not such figures as these but their followers. Many want to be gods, but who would be a slave? The derangement of Jones was manifest, yet so many members of his flock seemed normal, average, middle-class. One of his followers, a woman named Jann Gurvich, came from an affluent New Orleans background and attended the best schools. Like other young people in the late sixties, she became interested both in leftist politics and in religions that offered spiritual liberation, yet she brought an uncommon devotion to these interests. "By the fall of 1974, she was into Zen Buddhism, spending hours meticulously studying Sanskrit.... 'I had really gotten excited by the Upanishads and started studying Hindi and Sanskrit,'" she wrote about this period in her life. "'Later I was to get enthralled with Maoism and study Mandarin for a year and a half.'" She decided to go to India to study with Paramahamsa Yogananda but dropped these plans when she learned that Yogananda was dead (even though his school was still going). This change of plans plus a comment she made at the time tells a great deal about the kind of person who would submit themselves completely to a madman like Jones. "'I remember distinctly that I was in search of a teacher-- The Teacher--and from all I'd read I expected to find him in India. Instead, I found Jim Jones.'"[19]

That rigidly organized sects appeal to certain personality types and not to others is undeniable.  In her account
of her life in the Jehovah's Witnesses, Barbara Grizzuti Har-
rison notes that

> the Witnesses' appeal to victims, to the marginal,
> the exploited, the disenfranchised, is inestimable.
> Millenarian movements, sociologists say, do not
> appeal to those who are integrated into cohesive
> existing frameworks.  They burgeon in times of
> social disorder and cultural conflict when social
> controls are eroded, when the center does not hold
> --among those who feel themselves to be aliens
> and outsiders. [20]

For someone like Jann Gurvich, who not only had every advantage but also a propensity for leftist-liberationist beliefs,
the switch to a "teacher" like Jones suggests a personal un-
rest that expresses itself in social terms.  After canceling
her trip to India, Jann entered law school in California but
alienated many of her fellow students through her posturing.
"It was as if she did not know who she was."[21]

It is easy to psychoanalyze in the case of one person
like Jann Gurvich and to generalize with masses of people
like the followers of Jones or Kurtz, but certainly one element that may be lacking in many such instances is a sense
of personal worth.  In his film Apocalypse Now, so heavily
reliant on Heart of Darkness as its source, Francis Ford
Coppola emphasizes even more strongly than Conrad the baffling matter of discipleship.  In the film, a Captain Willard
is sent to a remote jungle outpost in Vietnam to kill the rene-
gade officer, also named Kurtz, who has abandoned the official U.S. mission and created a private empire protected by
an army of the faithful.  Willard is not the first sent out to
kill Kurtz, however.  He is preceded by a Lieutenant Colby,
who, like Willard, has been trained as an assassin.  But
somehow Colby has not only failed to follow orders but in
fact has enlisted with Kurtz and become part of his private
army.  He sends a letter to his wife, which is intercepted
by military authorities; scrawled in an erratic hand, it says,
"Sell the house, sell the kids, find someone else, I'm never
coming back."  There is no attempt made in the film to account for Colby's conversion, but a hired killer could hardly
be someone with a very strong sense of personal worth.  Poet
Tess Gallagher writes, "the ultimate sign of our disbelief in
our own souls is our inability to believe in the souls of any-

thing else. "[22] Someone with a deep sense of inadequacy is always fair game for a Jones or a Kurtz (the novelistic as well as the filmic version), no matter what their beliefs or actions have been in the past.

A significant part of the conditioning to which Jones regularly subjected his flock was the infamous White Night ritual, the fake mass suicide that became real at the end. [23] A typical White Night went like this:

> In the middle of the night, there would be rifle fire. The siren would sound the alarm. The loud-speaker would blare: "Everyone to the pavilion! We're under attack!" Frightened members would tumble out of bunks and stagger along the dirt paths to the main pavilion. There Jones would stand, looking grim. "There are CIA mercenaries out there, waiting to destroy us." Explaining in grave tones that the situation was hopeless, he would order a "White Night." The tub would be brought out, solemnly. Members would line up and resignedly drink. They were told they had but forty-five minutes to live. Then it was over. The flock, dazed, would wander back to their bunks and try to sleep with the fright: will I or will I not wake up? After a while, many of them no longer cared; some even hoped they wouldn't. White Night happened at least twice a month, more frequently if Jones couldn't sleep. [24]

In 1978, a People's Temple member named Deborah Blakey submitted an affidavit to the U.S. State Department in which she described the effect of the White Night drills. "'Life at Jonestown was so miserable and the physical pain of exhaustion so great that this event was not traumatic to me,'" said Blakey. "'I had become indifferent as to whether I lived or died.'"[25] In general, the acquiescence of the Temple members was simply "the supreme act of giving up, action taken in bad faith, underlining a sense of their own worthlessness.... They were simply exhausted with all the pressures and had come to wish for the end."[26] The built-in instability of a regime like this one stems from the fact that a Jones not only needs converts who feel worthless in the first place but also must work to maintain that sense of worthlessness through such rituals as the White Night drills. These drills, which recall the "'midnight dances ending with unspeakable rites'" arranged by Kurtz for his followers, were intense but short-lived, like the reign of Jones himself. They were unmistakably effective, of course, in that they reinforced the already-present self-hate that is the <u>sine qua non</u> of suicide. One feels an inarticulate sorrow upon realizing that the faithful thought themselves bad, so bad that they could never be good again except through their Teacher. Too, this sorrow is accompanied by a rage at the waste, the futility of it all. The next chapter in this study contains a discussion of existentialism, a modern philosophy with ancient roots and one that echoes a theme we have been studying all along--that each being is a cipher, a small void that participates in the larger one. In essence, no one is saint or sinner, hero or villain. How can we be bad or good when we are nothing at all?

Kurtz became a god to the wretched natives he exploited, approaching them "'"with the might as of a deity,"'" but in order to increase the distance between himself and his subjects, he had not only to heighten his own stature but continually diminish theirs. In the end, Marlow believes that Kurtz attains self-knowledge; trying to salvage some good from this terrible history, Marlow seizes what Kurtz has learned about "man's inhumanity to man" and passes it on in the form of a delirious epithet, the last words uttered by Kurtz before he is carried off by his final illness--"'The horror! The horror!'" After centuries of exposure to the Faust story in all its forms, as well as such real-life dramas as the Jonestown story, we can hardly be surprised to hear once again that playing God always leads to horror, especially when it entails the systematic degradation of others. But what Marlow misses, or at least what he fails to dwell upon for the instruction of his audience on the <u>Nellie,</u> is that just before Kurtz utters his memorable and oft-quoted words, he offers the only possible way to avoid the horror. What he says is, "'Live rightly, die, die.'"[27] Now "die, die" sounds rather threatening to Western ears, and no doubt it has an especially seditious ring to the ears of a Director, a Lawyer, an Accountant, all of whom want to extend life as they know it to the ignorant and the benighted. But a "meditating Buddha" like Marlow should know that we are all going to die anyway, so why not live rightly now?

---

"Here, at least, I could try to think
things out in peace, or, if not in peace,
in quiet. "

In the last four chapters, we examined monistic and quietistic elements in four works of literature, noting the ways in
which they combine with the more traditional and visible dualistic elements to which we are accustomed.  In so doing, we
enhanced our previous understanding of these works (and perhaps, in some cases, we overcame completely our earlier
misunderstanding of the works in question) by bringing to
them elements that often seem hidden yet are always present
in our culture.  In this chapter, we shall examine contemporary versions of monistic and quietistic patterns that have ex-
isted previously, as well as new forms that seem peculiar to
our times.  Our subjects will include Kenneth Rexroth, a once
vitriolic and highly political poet who seems to have meta-
morphosed into a nearly monastic (if not monistic) one; J. D.
Salinger, perhaps the most intelligent and sensitive of the
writers who capitalized on the Beat Zen phenomena of the
1950s and 1960s; Joyce Carol Oates, whose novel Unholy
Loves is a continuation of the Jamesian concern with detachment; and Ralph Ellison and Mark Strand, a novelist and a
poet whose works are elucidated by an understanding of existentialism, the West's most Easterly doctrine.

★

Kenneth Rexroth's latest collection of short lyrics and translations, The Morning Star, could easily be mistaken for a
book by a Japanese poet rather than an American one.  The
first section consists of very short poems, glimpses of the
natural world:

Orange and silver
Twilight over Yoshino.
Then the frosty stars,
Moving like crystals against
The wind from Siberia.

and

On the forest path
The leaves fall. In the withered
Grass the crickets sing
Their last songs. Through dew and dusk
I walk the paths you once walked,
My sleeves wet with memory. [1]

What is attempted in these short, untitled poems is
the directness and clarity more commonly associated with
Eastern than with Western art. The haiku poet Noboru Fujiwara says that his purpose is the discovery of essences, "a
weeding out of all that would clutter, muddy, confuse, leading
to great incisiveness, clear purpose." [2] So it is with Rexroth
in The Morning Star.

The directness of these poems can be seen in their
avoidance of traditional Western uses of imagery and symbol.
Reviewing Rexroth's One Hundred Poems from the Chinese,
William Carlos Williams comments on the absence of metaphor in Oriental verse. Metaphor is more at home in cultures where the dualistic nature of things is taken for granted,
for metaphor consists of an object and its reference--flint and
steel, says Williams, which spark when struck together. [3]

Too, despite the occasional human presence in these
poems, there seems to be as little of Rexroth himself here
as there is of metaphor, and this, too, is understandable
from an Oriental perspective. In A Meditator's Diary, Jane
Hamilton-Merritt recalls her discussions of the creative process with a Thai monk, who pointed out that the truly religious
do not write at all, much less parade their own egos for the
world's admiration. [4]

The second section of The Morning Star is a meditation
on mortality and eternity. The third, a translated sequence
called "The Love Poems of Marichiko," forms what Rexroth
calls "a sort of little novel." The strongest of the three
sections, these poems dwell on the delights of passionate

and illicit love. To the Eastern mind, writes Joseph Campbell in Myths to Live By, only illicit love is passionate, and certainly it is passionate here. [5]

> I scream as you bite
> My nipples, and orgasm
> Drains my body, as if I
> Had been cut in two.

and

> Your tongue thrums and moves
> Into me, and I become
> Hollow and blaze with
> Whirling light, like the inside
> Of a vast expanding pearl.

and

> As I came from the
> Hot bath, you took me before
> The horizontal mirror
> Beside the low bed, while my
> Breasts quivered in your hands, my
> Buttocks shivered against you. [6]

But as the Buddha says, "The combinations of the world are unstable by nature," and the affair ends badly:

> Chilled through, I wake up
> With the first light. Outside my window
> A red maple leaf floats silently down.
> What am I to believe?
> Indifference?
> Malice?
> I hate the sight of coming day
> Since that morning when
> Your insensitive gaze turned me to ice
> Like the pale moon in the dawn. [7]

The tone throughout The Morning Star is one of quietism; the passion in "The Love Poems of Marichiko" simply throws into relief the solitary, minimal, introspective nature of Rexroth's persona. How different these 1979 poems are from those written by the Rexroth of the 1944 collection The Phoenix and the Tortoise, whose bold assertiveness recalls that of Lawrence and Pound and Whitman. [8] The tranquillity of the voice in The Morning Star contrasts sharply with the one we hear in "Thou Shalt Not Kill: A Memorial for Dylan Thomas" (which appears in the 1956 collection In Defense of the Earth):

> And all the birds of the deep sea rise up
> Over the luxury liners and scream,
> "You killed him! You killed him.
> In your God damned Brooks Brothers suit,
> You son of a bitch."9

In those days, Rexroth sounded like a nabi, a term that he himself applied to Allen Ginsberg, denoting one of those bearded, bad-smelling crazies who came down from the hills to Jerusalem periodically and denounced everyone.10 (Or, less exotically, Rexroth was simply an "old-fashioned American sorehead," to borrow Alfred Kazin's phrase.11) But today he appears to belong, or to want to belong, at least as much as a publishing writer can, to the Buddhist bodhisattvas or the yamabushi of Japan or the zaddiks of Hasidism or the Shi'ite hidden imam of Islam. These are Rexroth's heros, as one sees from his prose writings and from an interview with him in an American Buddhist magazine called Zero; their goal is to ignore the world, to "live unknown."12 One might characterize this change with Rexroth's own words from his essay on Rimbaud: "True illumination always results in a special sweetness of temper, a deep, lyric equanimity and magnanimity. The outstanding characteristic of the mystic's vision is that it is satisfying. He is never frustrated, at least not in our worldly sense."13

Various reasons can be given for this change in Rexroth's outlook; that he simply "saw the light" is sufficient and no doubt at least partly true. But the mere fact of aging must be taken into account here, and if we are to discuss monism and quietism as practical outlooks rather than abstract ones, we are forced to admit that they are more commonly associated with age than with youth. To put it another way, we must recognize the futility of counseling detachment and withdrawal to the young, a theme treated by writers of all sorts throughout the centuries. Augustine's Confessions mark the difference between the priestly old man and the younger one who prayed, "Give me chastity and continence, but not just now."14 Clarence Darrow said, "Anyone who is an optimist after thirty is a fool, and anyone who is a pessimist before thirty is too damned smart."15 According to the English biographer Hesketh Pearson, "The youth of twenty who does not think the world can be improved is a cad; the man of forty who still thinks it can is a fool."[16] Ariel Durant, in accounting for the change in her social views and those of her husband, intellectual historian Will Durant, gives two reasons for their gradual switch from advocating armed violence against the state to principled concern: "fifty-five years and a rising income."[17] While Rexroth was an important figure in the contemporary Zen movement in the United States, then, his present tendencies toward monism and quietism in his poetry may reflect angry youth's tendency to become mellow age rather than specific religious or philosophical beliefs.

I would expect the type of poetry gathered in The Morning Star to appeal to adolescents, not because of the themes but because of its "easiness," just as I would expect these same poems to be anathema to university undergraduates reared on T. S. Eliot. But this same "easy" poetry that will appeal to young readers who have read nothing should prove attractive as well to older readers who have read much. In an essay on "The Literature of Replenishment," John Barth suggests that very complex contemporary works are best appreciated, not by narrow specialists, but by those who have read widely and generously. Might not the same be said for very simple works? Barth writes, "If modernist works are often forbidding and require a fair amount of help and training to appreciate, it does not follow that they are not superbly rewarding, as climbing Mount Matterhorn must be, or sailing a small boat around the world."[18] The same is true of works that are not at all forbidding and require no help and training whatsoever to appreciate, even though the appreciation of them is aided immensely if one's reading habits are liberal. No one who has been restricted to neighborhood rambles would consider the Matterhorn, but readers who have been to the mountaintop might be glad to find "a deep, lyric equanimity and magnanimity" when they come down.

★

The intrusion of the Orient in Western thought is markedly recurrent, especially in America.[19] The first phase of influence derives largely from the work of the British and European comparative mythologists and philosophers who were contemporaries of the early nineteenth-century New England Transcendentalists and Romantics; this phase culminates in the poems of Whitman. The second, or fin de siècle, phase is seen in the art of Whistler, the prose of Lafcadio Hearn, and the translations of Ernest Fenollosa. And the third phase is seen primarily in the impact of Zen Buddhism on the mid-twentieth-century Beat movement in American letters.

By any measure, Zen received an ambivalent reception from American intellectuals. The difficulty is compounded in trying to gauge the effect of a thoroughly Eastern practice like Zen on a thoroughly Western author like J. D. Salinger, and the resultant confusion, ineptness, and outright hostility is evident in the writings of some of his most sympathetic critics. Warren French, for example, author of the most widely used monograph on Salinger, notes the presence of Zen in Salinger's work but adds "there is no indication that Salinger really grasps the principles of this paradox-ridden Oriental cult."20 (One wonders if French is equally dismissive of the Jewish and Christian "cults.")

There is less xenophobia in other critical studies; Gerald Rosen, for example, has devoted a small monograph to the subject of Zen in the Art of J. D. Salinger. Oddly, though, Rosen says very little about Franny and Zooey, in which the principles of Zen are discussed outright, and gives almost all of his attention to The Catcher in the Rye. However, an understanding of The Catcher in the Rye is necessary if one is to grasp Salinger's fuller development of Zen ideas in Franny and Zooey. Rosen notes the parallels between the Buddha's experience and that of Holden Caulfield. Both are shielded from the world; both are appalled when they enter the world and discover old age, sickness, and death; both set out in search of a guide and fail to find one. From this low point, the Buddha works out his own salvation based on detachment and withdrawal from the world and then he returns to the world out of compassion for his fellow sufferers. "In rough outline," says Rosen, "and without the Buddha's final conscious mature understanding, this is the form of the story of Holden Caulfield."21

Bernice and Sanford Goldstein bring more insight to the matter as they see in The Catcher in the Rye the "germ" of Franny and Zooey. To the Goldsteins, Holden is the ancestor of the surviving Glass children. Like them (and like much of mid-century American intelligentsia), he is overly rational, overly critical. He finds that his constant analysis and rejection of everyone he meets in the course of the novel establishes an unhealthy distance between himself and the world. Thus, at the novel's end, he misses even those who are his former tormentors, including the pimp Maurice, who has beaten him up. By creating a character who rejects the

world's ugliness and then finds that he is unhappy without it,
Salinger sets the stage for the Glass children, who are, according to the Goldsteins, "fully endowed and fully aware and
fully self-conscious and quite unhappy." Unlike Holden, though,
the Glasses end up at least "partially enlightened," or, to use
the Goldsteins' felicitous turn of phrase, they attain "a twentieth-century American form of enlightenment."[22]

My own reading of Franny and Zooey accepts Salinger's use of Zen but sees in it nothing that conflicts with our
Western traditions of monism and quietism. Blake says that
the soul passes from innocence through experience to higher
innocence. In his Divine Comedy, Dante passes from mortal
life through the Inferno to Paradise. At one point in his life,
Hawthorne thought of writing an allegory that depicted the
heart as sunny at the exterior, sinister in the interior, and
Edenic at the core.[23] This paradigm is sometimes stripped
of its religious and literary implications and made to serve
in other contexts. For instance, the philosopher Alfred North
Whitehead uses it to justify a rigorous education when he says
that the student goes from freedom through discipline to higher
freedom. No matter how the paradigm is used, however, the
point is that one must go through Hell or experience or whatever it is called--something analogous to the suffering of the
Buddha, in other words--before attaining the higher state.

Franny and Zooey describes the attempts of the late
Seymour Glass and his brother Buddy to spare Franny and
Zooey, their younger sister and brother, the trauma of experience. This they do by pushing the literature of the higher
innocence upon Franny and Zooey when the children are too
young to see its necessity. As Buddy says in a letter to
Zooey,

> "We wanted you both to know who and what Jesus
> and Gautama and Lao-Tse and Shankaracharya and
> Hui-neng and Sri Ramakrishna, etc., were before
> you knew too much or anything about Homer or
> Shakespeare or even Blake or Whitman, let alone
> George Washington and his cherry tree or the defi-
> nition of a peninsula or how to parse a sentence."[24]

But all this early knowledge does is make Franny and
Zooey into freaks. As Zooey says, "'I'm a twenty-five-year-
old freak and she's a twenty-year-old freak, and both those
bastards are responsible.'"[25] When Franny's spiritual col-
lapse comes, she explains it in the language of Jesus, Gautama,
and Seymour and Buddy Glass:

"Everything everybody does is so--I don't know--not wrong, or even mean, or even stupid necessarily. But just so tiny and meaningless and--sad-making.... I used to hate myself so, when I was in a play, to be backstage after the play was over. All those egos running around feeling terribly charitable and warm.... I'm just sick of ego, ego, ego. My own and everybody else's. I'm sick of everybody that wants to get somewhere, do something distinguished and all, be somebody interesting."26

When Lane, her boyfriend, asks Franny if she isn't simply afraid of competing, she replies, "'I'm not afraid to compete. It's just the opposite. Don't you see that? I'm afraid I will compete--that's what scares me.'"27 Franny understands her unhappiness intellectually but she has not lived through it yet. Further, she expects her understanding to help her through the crisis; because she has been indoctrinated with the teachings of the sages, she expects that knowledge to lift her out of her misery. But knowledge alone is never enough, especially for the young and inexperienced, as we have already seen in The Mill on the Floss. Besides, as the examples from Blake, Dante, Hawthorne, Alfred North Whitehead, and the life of the Buddha suggest, true misery precedes true knowledge and not vice versa. Franny knows the language of the higher innocence; she has a kind of formula for redemption, the celebrated Jesus Prayer, and she repeats it endlessly. But she cannot experience the higher innocence because she has not experienced experience.

Freaks, to define Zooey's term, are people who speak the language of Heaven even though they live in Hell, where, of course, they cannot be understood, even by themselves. Thus, when Franny is rescued from the hell of her own problems, it is by a kind of literary act rather than a spiritual or psychological one. What saves Franny is Zooey's translation of the message of Jesus, Gautama, and Seymour and Buddy Glass into the language of his and Franny's common experience. He tells her that as a child radio star he used to shine his shoes at Seymour's insistence because the Fat Lady might be listening to the broadcast that day. At first, Zooey did not understand what Seymour meant, but gradually he came to realize that everybody is the Fat Lady, sweaty and cancerous, and that the Fat Lady herself is Jesus Christ. In its abstractness, the Jesus Prayer does nothing for Franny. It is not Christ the Son of God we must understand and serve, it is Christ the Fat Lady--not a distant deity, in other words,

but humankind in all its splendor and repulsiveness. When
Franny realizes this, it seems to her "as if all of what little
or much wisdom there is in the world were suddenly hers,"
and she lies quietly smiling for a while before drifting into
"a deep, dreamless sleep."[28]

★

Joyce Carol Oates has received an extraordinary amount of
critical attention, much of it negative. Praised and damned
in equal measure, her work seems to invite every approach,
every application of any critical yardstick whatsoever. If
there is one thing her critics have in common, however, it
is a tendency to link her to the past, to see her work as an
updating of old themes.

> Don't let her fool you with stunt styles and timely
> touches. Keep your eye on her standard Victorian
> plots, observe the carefully presented poetry of her
> prose. Joyce Carol Oates is an anachronism: the
> last of the 19th Century Gothic novelists, the fourth
> Brontë sister. [29]

> For her emphasis on self-seeking ferocity we call
> Oates "Gothic," but she is perhaps better understood
> as a contemporary heir of the Great Tradition. Like
> Austen, Eliot, or James in their various ways, but
> with a gift for violence, she aligns the moral and
> the social. [30]

> Like the most important modern writers--Joyce,
> Proust, Mann--she has an absolute identification
> with her material: the spirit of a society at a
> crucial point in its history. [31]

A recent novel by Oates, Unholy Loves, despite its contemporary surface, has roots that sink deeply into the past. Unholy Loves is an academic novel, which is to say that it belongs to a genre whose main purpose is to expose and titillate.
From a book like Alison Lurie's enormously popular The War
Between the Tates, millions of ordinary Americans learned
that academics were not the goody-goodies they sometimes
seemed to be--that they were, instead, very much like ordinary Americans in that they too slugged their spouses, failed
to use dental floss twice a day, and engaged in sexual practices rather far afield from those recommended by the Old
Testament. But Unholy Loves, despite a title that should

cause charge cards to all but spring from billfolds as if of their own volition, is an academic novel of a rather different sort, since it participates in the tradition of monism and quietism that is older than literature itself.

There is less of a paradox at work here than one might think. Oates has her own reasons for making academe the subject of her scrutiny. It is not necessarily a matter of her writing about what she knows best, since she has written effectively on a number of subjects, or of her making a special pitch to a reliable market, since academics, who are used to getting free examination copies, are notoriously stingy when it actually comes to buying books themselves. In Unholy Loves, Oates seems primarily interested in the workings of the mind. So, just as Zola went to the dram shops of Paris when he wanted to study depravity, Oates goes to a university, a setting uniquely suited to her purpose not only because good minds are found there but also because nowhere else is the mind allowed the time, the freedom, and the silence in which to turn inward, to examine and then to purify or debase itself.

The school in question is that distinguished if fictional institution Woodslee University, located in an icy hinterland hundreds of miles north of New York City, a place as isolated as a moon base or a gulag in Solzhenitsyn's archipelago. And what ugliness we find there! Everyone wants a piece of Albert St. Dennis, visiting Distinguished Professor of Poetry, a drunken, garrulous old man out of Balzac, a decaying Englishman whose enormous achievement means less to him than it does to everyone else on the Woodslee faculty. Professor Lewis Seidel, for instance, hopes that St. Dennis will dedicate his next book to him, calling Seidel "the American Socrates" or perhaps "the American Nietzsche" or simply "my American friend"; the problem is that St. Dennis cannot remember Seidel's name.[32] Even Brigit Stott, Woodslee's resident novelist and the novel's heroine, wonders if St. Dennis will not be one of her "holy loves."

The novel's title comes from Augustine's Confessions ("To Carthage then I came, where a cauldron of unholy loves sang all about mine ears"). The idea seems to be that most loves are unholy, a notion with which one might concur if Alexis Kessler, a composer on the Woodslee faculty and Brigit's eventual lover, is any example. Kessler is one of the most repulsive characters in modern fiction. He wears jewels and perfume and he bleaches his hair, but when Brigit remarks innocently on their first meeting that his hands are dirty, he says, "'If you think my hands are dirty, lady, you should see the rest of me.'"[33]

Sometimes love is where you find it, however, and before long Brigit and Kessler are carrying on like undergraduates, even if Brigit can make no progress on the novel she wants to write. Their love fails, and St. Dennis dies in a fire, events not totally unexpected in a book as full of foreboding as Flaubert's Madame Bovary. For just as Emma Bovary is shadowed by a tramp with a sardonic song, so the characters in Unholy Loves are mocked by Leslie Cullendon, a young faculty member who is dying from a mysterious disease and who becomes more shrill and bitter as his condition worsens. Along the same line, there is Brigit's surly and senile grandfather and, finally, a desperate, disheveled stranger who interrupts and nearly ruins a dinner party in a very minor scene, one that is all the more disturbing because it has no discernible connection to the narrative and thus reinforces the idea that life is ultimately senseless.

These minor characters and events remind us that the world is something we should not ignore, since it certainly will not ignore us. After St. Dennis dies, Brigit recalls that certain philosophers think of the universe as an entity that exists only in God's mind and that if God stops thinking about it for an instant, the universe will sink into oblivion. So it is with individuals, she realizes; she must invent herself anew at each moment or she will be engulfed by the ugliness, the random chaos that surrounds her. So she cultivates detachment. Miraculously, her novel begins almost to write itself. Kessler, who has left Woodslee after St. Dennis's death, returns determined both to make something of himself (he too has been creatively bankrupt for some time) and to reclaim Brigit as a lover. But she refuses him. The book ends with them talking friendlily though guardedly and from opposite standpoints, for he wants everything and has nothing, while she wants nothing and has it all.

A tenet common to monistic philosophies is that the most desirable mental state is one that is tranquil yet aware, while the least desirable state of mind is one that is agitated and unseeing. This idea is present in both The Confessions of St. Augustine and Madame Bovary, as well as a third book that stands behind Unholy Loves as clearly as these two. It is Henry James's The Wings of the Dove, a novel that Brigit thinks of as "James's most beautiful work" but also "an exquisite, maddening riddle never satisfactorily explained."[34]

Unholy Loves ends exactly as does The Wings of the Dove,
with two lovers recognizing that they can never be lovers
again, or, as Brigit thinks in another context, that "magic
might depart from every experience."[35] But at least the
magic is there at some point, if only we are sufficiently calm
and focused to see it.

Oddly enough, it is not the failure of her love affair
with Kessler that brings Brigit around. Harrowing though
that failure is, it is less consequential than St. Dennis's
death, even though the old man was more or less a stranger
to her as he was to everyone else at Woodslee. But it is
his death rather than the failure of love that suggests to her
that life is inherently unfair and therefore must be lived
mindfully. Love has its place, Oates seems to be saying,
but death is the great teacher.

★

William Barrett gives us a vivid picture of the birth of existentialism:

> While [Kierkegaard] sat one Sunday afternoon in the
> Fredriksberg Garden in Copenhagen smoking a cigar
> as was his habit, and turning over a great many
> things in his mind, he suddenly reflected that he
> had as yet made no career for himself whereas
> everywhere around him he saw the men of his age
> becoming celebrated, establishing themselves as
> renowned benefactors of mankind. They were bene-
> factors because all their efforts were directed at
> making life easier for the rest of mankind, whether
> materially by constructing railroads, steamboats,
> or telegraph lines, or intellectually by publishing
> easy compendiums to universal knowledge, or--most
> audacious of all--spiritually by showing how thought
> could make spiritual existence systematically easier
> and easier. Kierkegaard's cigar burned down, he
> lighted another, the train of reflection held him.
> It occurred to him then that since everyone was
> engaged everywhere in making things easy, perhaps
> someone might be needed to make things hard again;
> that life might become so easy that people would
> want the difficult back again; and that this might be
> a career and destiny for him.[36]

Actually, the reference books tell us that the word "existentialism" can apply to several different and even conflicting philosophical systems. Its importance to this study, however, is that existentialism in general represents a disillusionment with the smug world disdained by Kierkegaard and with "the secular and religious laws or abstractions that make a man not a passionately deciding, spiritual being, but a passionlessly conforming, cog-like being, incapable of deep feeling, incapable of his own spiritual or moral choices."37 In defining Kierkegaard's opposition to the "Public Thing" or Res Publica, many of his explicators make this Western philosopher sound like a Buddhist. For example, "For Kierkegaard paradox, contradiction, releases minds from neat, orderly, publicly persuasive arguments, and frees us for passionate, isolated decision-making."38 If, as opposed to neat laws and abstractions, there is nothing but Nothing, if there is only death at the end of life, then Kierkegaard's insistence of the importance of isolated, examined existence is clearly related to our study of monism and quietism.

According to Barrett,

> Human moods and reactions to the encounter with Nothingness vary considerably from person to person, and from culture to culture. The Chinese Taoists found the Great Void tranquilizing, peaceful, even joyful. For the Buddhists in India, the idea of Nothing evoked a mood of universal compassion for all creatures caught in the toils of an existence that is ultimately groundless. In the traditional culture of Japan the idea of Nothingness pervades the exquisite modes of aesthetic feeling displayed in painting, architecture, and even the ceremonial rituals of daily life. But Western man, up to his neck in things, objects, and the business of mastering them, recoils with anxiety from any possible encounter with Nothingness and labels talk of it as "negative"--which is to say, morally reprehensible. 39

Not all Westerners feel this way, of course, as the remarks on Kierkegaard suggest, as well as the comments in Chapter 1 on the thought of Schopenhauer and Freud. For many existentialists, says Barrett, "the Self, indeed, is in Sartre's treatment, as in Buddhism, a bubble, and a bubble has nothing at its center."40 The surface of that Self-bubble consists of what I do: I put on a suit, I take my sons to school, I have breakfast at such-and-such a restaurant, I meet my classes, I work on this book, and so on. At the center of that bubble is nothing--me, the me that is me and is everyone else, too, since we are all the same nothing.  Paradoxically, though, to realize this connection we must separate ourselves from the world, which is why Epictetus advised us to live unknown, why the Sakyamuni disdained politics, why Kierkegaard counseled implacable opposition to the Res Publica, why, according to Thomas à Kempis, you should "keep yourself a stranger and pilgrim upon the earth, to whom the affairs of this world are no concern."[41]

Kierkegaard did his work well, but it took the events of the twentieth century to bring his seed to fruition.  As a philosophy for daily living, existentialism transcends its esoteric, pre-Kierkegaardian origins because it offers an answer to madness that has never before operated on a global scale. Hence, the applicability of a philosophy to so many other forms of expression.  It is safe to say that without Hitler, Mussolini, economic depression, and the dehumanizing effects of industrialization and technology, we would not have the plays of Ionesco and Beckett, the music of Nono, Boulez, Henze, and Stockhausen, the films of Chabrol, Truffaut, Godard, Rivette, and Resnais, Abstract Expressionism, and the nouveau roman.  Speaking of the period just after World War II, Christopher Butler, a critic of the avant-garde, notes:

> There is of course a more general influence of existentialism in this transitional period:  and it is a moral one.  It provided a sense of purpose which was necessary for recovery from the fascist period, and gave confidence to the avant-garde.  Its long-term effects, however, seem to me to belong more to the history of liberalism than to experimental art.  The moral assumptions of existentialism did indeed underlie the principles of much "avant-garde" psychiatry in our period (in Rollo May or R. D. Laing) but they come through most clearly in liberal novel writing.  Herzog, My Life as a Man, Portnoy's Complaint, Something Happened, let alone Mailer's American Dream and "White Negro" hipsterism can, it seems to me, be best understood as peculiarly existentialist forms of confession, and the same applies to much of the work of Berryman and Lowell. Indeed the individual's independent, often anti-ideological search for value ... underlies far more than the artistic work of the post-war period.  To parody Edward VII, "We are all existentialists now."[42]

Ralph Ellison's Invisible Man begins with an epigraph from Melville's Benito Cereno: "'You are saved,' cried Captain Delano, more and more astonished and pained; 'you are saved: what has cast such a shadow upon you?'"[43] Captain Delano has in fact saved Benito Cereno from his crew of mutinous slaves, but instead of being joyous, Delano sinks into a deep depression and dies as much of melancholy as of anything else. Ellison does not give Cereno's reply to Delano in the epigraph; what casts such a shadow on Cereno is, in his own words, "'The negro.'" Alone among the members of his class, Cereno has known what it is to be a slave, to be under the domination of another race. Yet he knows that he cannot put his experiences into words and that, even if he does, the slave business, with its ties to the economic system of the entire New World, will go on anyway. Isolated among his peers, trapped in the midst of freedom by his horrifying realization, Cereno can do nothing but fix upon the cause of his misery and eventual death. His paralysis foreshadows much of the static, fixated hopelessness in twentieth-century fiction: the impotence of Jake Barnes in The Sun Also Rises; Gatsby's insistence that Daisy loves him as much as she did before the war in The Great Gatsby; the pathetic clinging of the Compson family to plantation virtues in The Sound and the Fury. What makes the story of Invisible Man different is its protagonist's gradual exfoliation or stripping away of the identities that are forced upon him until he stands alone in splendid, contemplative, self-affirming silence.

The nameless protagonist's story may be seen as a kind of meditation on success. His initial exposure to the idea is conventional; he must engage in a boxing match, scramble for money on an electrified mat, and give a censored speech in order to please the men who are underwriting his education. In other words, he accepts a tolerable amount of unpleasantness in order to attain a truly worthwhile goal. Once in college, however, he learns that there is more to life than is suggested by this simple formula. He sees a sharp contrast between the wealthy Mr. Norton, who honors his dead daughter's memory by helping the underprivileged, and the shiftless Trueblood, who has begotten a baby on his own daughter. As Trueblood's lot has improved since his moral lapse (he receives charity from those who ignored him before), the irony of the contrast is not lost on Norton, either. He has a fit of sorts and is taken into a roadhouse, The Golden Day, which is patronized by disturbed World War I veterans from a nearby hospital. Just as there was an implicit contrast between Norton and Trueblood, there is an implicit comparison between the now-helpless philanthropist and these veterans. "Many of the men had been doctors, lawyers, teachers, Civil Service workers," thinks the protagonist; "there were several cooks, a preacher, a politician, and an artist. One very nutty one had been a psychiatrist. Whenever I saw them I felt uncomfortable. They were supposed to be members of the professions toward which at various times I vaguely aspired myself."[44] The roadhouse itself seems to have participated in this inversion of the social order in which the high are made low and vice versa; when Norton asks what the building was used for in the past, the bartender replies, " 'It was a church, then a bank, then it was a restaurant and a fancy gambling house, and now we got it.' "[45]

For his part in allowing Norton to become excited and sick, the protagonist is expelled from college, but not before the president, Dr. Bledsoe, furthers his education on the difference between appearance and reality. Seemingly a docile figure who kowtows to his white benefactors, Bledsoe not only controls boys like the protagonist but men like Norton as well.

> "You're nobody, son. You don't exist--can't you
> see that? The white folk tell everybody what to
> think--except men like me. I tell them; that's my
> life, telling white folks how to think about the things
> I know about. Shocks you, doesn't it? Well, that's
> the way it is. It's a nasty deal and I don't always
> like it myself. But you listen to me: I didn't
> make it, and I know that I can't change it. But
> I've made my place in it and I'll have every Negro
> in the country hanging on tree limbs by morning
> if it means staying where I am.... This is a power
> set-up, son, and I'm at the controls. You think
> about that. When you buck against me, you're
> bucking against power, rich white folk's power,
> the nation's power, which means government power!"[46]

The government is a father (it sets rules for us and it "helps" us when we need it), and indeed Invisible Man is a book full of fathers, from the men who send the protagonist away to college to Bledsoe to Norton himself, who is associated with such male power figures as General Pershing, St. Nicholas, John D. Rockefeller, and Thomas Jefferson, a Founding Father.[47] The most important advice the protagonist will receive (although it requires several hundred pages before he

understands it) comes from one of the babylike veterans, who
says, " 'Now is the time for offering fatherly advice ... but
I'll have to spare you that--since I guess I'm nobody's father
except my own. Perhaps that's the advice to give you: Be
your own father, young man. '"48

    In the course of this rich, dense novel, the protagonist
goes from father to father: his bosses at Liberty Paints, the
doctors who threaten castration and apply electroshock, the
leaders of the Brotherhood who are ostensibly his comrades
yet who are as restrictive and manipulative as the others.
At the height of his success as an orator for the Brotherhood,
he is more tightly controlled than ever before. He begins to
feel schizophrenic, then paranoid. His sanity is saved by the
loss of another's; when Brother Tod Clifton deserts the movement and is killed by a policeman he has deliberately pro-
voked, the protagonist wakes up and sees that the science of
the Brotherhood is no match for human nature. Clifton is
dead, yet the crowds go on as they have always done. "All
our work had been very little, no great change had been
made. And it was all my fault. I'd been so fascinated by
the motion that I'd forgotten to measure what it was bringing
forth. I'd been asleep, dreaming."49 Eulogizing Clifton, he
praises him not for his success or lack of it but for his humanity: " 'Here are the facts. He was standing and he fell.
He fell and he kneeled. He kneeled and he bled. He bled
and he died. He fell in a heap like any man and his blood
spilled out like any blood. '"50 To the brothers who condemn
Clifton because he left the movement, the protagonist says,
" 'He was a man and a Negro; a man and brother; a man and
a traitor, as you say; then he was a dead man, and alive or
dead he was jam-full of contradictions. '"51 The Brotherhood
tries to capitalize on Clifton's death by starting a riot, and
the protagonist is tugged this way and that, both by the war-
ring factions of his own loyalties. At the end, however, he
realizes "that it was better to live out one's own absurdity
than to die for that of others."52

    Rather than death, however, the protagonist chooses
life--and invisibility. Driven into a coal cellar, he elects
to stay there and cultivate awareness. With "pain-sharpened
eyes" he sees that those who win the rat race are still rats
and thereby separate from humankind, whereas in reality "we,
through no fault of our own, were linked to all the others in
the loud, clamoring semi-visible world."53 It has occurred
to him "to return into that 'heart of darkness' across the
Mason-Dixon line, but then I remind myself that the true

darkness lies within my own mind, and the idea loses itself
in the gloom.... Here, at least, I could try to think things
out in peace, or, if not in peace, in quiet."⁵⁴

★

Insofar as free verse is able to wander in the manner of the
meditating mind, it may be said to have a generic advantage
over other literary forms in its treatment of monistic and
quietistic themes. (This assertion takes into account the assumed adequacy of other pertinent factors, such as the per-
ceptiveness and skill of the free-verse author, for instance.)
To understand why this is so, a glance at the history of verse
forms is necessary. Galway Kinnell tells us that rhyme and
meter were meant to imitate a supernatural harmony in the
seventeenth century, to "echo a celestial music"; though Kinnell gives no examples, a poem like Milton's "A Solemn Music" illustrates his point. In the eighteenth century, poetry
became very worldly, and outward form was seen as a cele-
bration of humankind's logical bent. As faith in both spiritual
matters and human perfection began to crumble with the Romantics and the Victorians, rhyme and meter started to "assume a far more energetic function, which is to call back,
in poetry, the grace disappearing from everything else."
Writers of the present day can have no illusions about the
disappearance of that grace, which is why, according to Kinnell,

> for modern poets--for everyone after Yeats--rhyme
> and meter amount to little more than mechanical
> aids for writing.... In rhyme and meter one has
> to be concerned with how to say something, perhaps
> anything, which fulfills the formal requirements.
> It is hard to move into the open that way. If you
> were walking through the woods in winter, rhyming
> would be like following those footprints continually
> appearing ahead of you in the snow. Fixed form
> tends to bring you to a place where someone has
> been before. Naturally, in a poem, you wish to
> reach a new place. That requires pure wandering.

The antediluvians who believe that nothing written after Yeats's
day is poetry are fond of invoking Robert Frost's simile about
free verse being like tennis played with the net down. Nice
analogy, says Kinnell, "except that the poem is not like a
game, but more resembles a battle or a journey, where there
are so many obstacles in the nature of the case that it would

be a kind of evasion to invent additional, purely arbitrary ones."55

However, one drawback of free verse is that without the external checks of rhyme and meter poets run the risk of all sounding alike, perhaps without even knowing it. In a recent issue of The Virginia Quarterly Review, Laura Jensen's poems are described as "the type that get published in The New Yorker and fine literary magazines; they have a subdued, personal voice masking a quiet intensity."56 This remark, so pithily descriptive of contemporary poetry in America, is no doubt meant entirely as praise. Yet so many poets have such subdued, quietly intense voices that they seem virtually indistinguishable. Worse, these poets lack a certain fundamental concreteness, the very de quoi that Emerson admired in Montaigne. (Emerson's reference is to the story of the cherubs who visited the archbishop. The courteous prelate said, "Asseyez-vous, mes enfants," but the incorporeal cherubs replied, "Monsieur, nous n'avons pas de quoi.") Mark Strand is not free of the charge of sounding distant and disembodied in his poetry. Nevertheless, he is the only poet writing today to capitalize on the idea of the quiet, personal voice and to make it not just a stance or pump-priming gimmick of some kind but the fertile ground of his thought and art.

A review of his career to date shows how true this is. Richard Howard, whose short essay on Strand in Alone with America: Essays on the Art of Poetry in the United States Since 1950 is the most perceptive commentary on Strand's first two books, notes that his Sleeping with One Eye Open is "a book of forebodings and apprehensions." The title poem ends this way: "And I lie sleeping with one eye open, /Hoping/That nothing, nothing will happen." In this first book, writes Howard, Strand "is holding on for dear life," and though I am more comfortable with the notion that it is a persona rather than the author himself who is holding on, I would agree that the poet, beneath his quiet surfaces, is "nervous and morbid" and in that way very much like any number of his peers.

All that changes in Reasons for Moving. In this collection, Strand's persona suggests that it is the Self who has been making trouble for him--again, something that other poets were saying at about the same time. Technically, and once more I paraphrase Howard's essay, Strand divided himself against himself in order to discover (or invent) the basis for his nervousness and morbidity; philosophically, Strand's persona discovers that je est un autre, as Rimbaud said. The persona copes with this meddlesome Self by treating it with black humor or, as in the title poem, with Roethkean mysticism: "In a field / I am the absence of field," etc. [57]

But black humor and mysticism are only first aid measures for Strand, court plaster on a psychic wound that needs more serious attention. In Darker, he has clearly abandoned the dualistic notion of joking the Self away or neutralizing it through mystical means. What he wants to do in this book is get rid of the Self, and in doing so he begins to separate himself definitively from the other quiet, personal, angst-ridden poets with identical concerns and identical ways of handling them. The poems in Darker are poems of self-dissolution. "I give up. I give up," he writes, "And you will have none of it because already I am beginning / again without anything." Yet this is positive self-negation. It renews: "I empty myself of my life and my life remains." [58] A little of that idea goes a long way, of course, and some of the poems have a sort of absenter-than-thou sound that can be cloying after a while.

But if Darker posits again and again the poet's program, in The Story of Our Lives the reader sees that program put into effect. To do so, Strand changed his style; in the words of the dust jacket, these poems are "longer, more mysterious, more engrossing" than Strand's earlier poems. There are only seven poems here. One of them is the magnificent "Elegy for My Father," which is one of the finest elegies in the English language and which is remarkable in the way that it distinguishes itself from "Lycidas" and "Adonais" and In Memoriam by being--as one might expect, given Strand's announced intent in Darker--more a poem of cleaning up and clearing out than these others are. The loss of a father is in part a loss of self, provided one is able to lose it. But that takes effort, effort that the persona makes: "Your shadow is yours," he tells his father. "I told it so. I said it was yours. / I have carried it with me too long. I give it back." [59] Like the others in this book, "Elegy for My Father" is an utterly convincing poem, disquietingly so. For these poems have a Möbius-strip quality to them; they remind one of the bird who flew around in smaller and smaller circles until he disappeared up his own backside. These poems seem to say, "This is it, this is final, this is all I know, all I can do." "The Untelling" is a poem in which the persona appears as a man with paper in his hand trying desper-

ately to bring to long-gone relatives his account of a day
with them, but the more he tries, the more he fails, and
the poem ends with his beginning to write it. On closing
The Story of Our Lives, the reader is well within rights to
ask, "Now what?"

The Monument provides the answer to that question.
It is dedicated "To the Translator of / THE MONUMENT /
in the future." This seems a rather presumptuous dedication,
especially for a poet of self-effacement. But from the very
beginning it is clear that Strand is playing another game entirely. The Monument is not quite poetry, not quite prose.
It consists of fifty-two short "chapters" that are partly statements by a persona, partly quotations from Octavio Paz, Mi-
guel de Unamuno, Wallace Stevens, Shakespeare, Wordsworth,
Sir Thomas Browne, Nietzsche, and others. The first chapter says, in its entirety, "Let me introduce myself. I am
... and so on and so forth. Now you know more about me
than I know about you." The persona is spoofing Descartes
here: you think, therefore I am. To write a book of this
kind is to run an enormous risk, of course, particularly in
the eyes of friends, enemies, and colleagues. "They would
mistake this modest document as self-centered in the ex-
treme," admits the persona, "not only because none of their
names appears in it, but because I have omitted mention of
my wife and daughter. How mistaken they are. This poor
document does not have to do with a self, it dwells on the
absence of a self." Elsewhere he elaborates: "The Monument is a void, artless and everlasting. What I was I am
no longer. I speak for nothing, the nothing that I am, the
nothing that is this work. And you shall perpetuate me not
in the name of what I was, but in the name of what I am."[60]

Students of the theory of translation are familiar with
the idea that some works do not achieve their full potential
until they are translated; for instance, I recall reading that,
to those who know the languages, Poe is better in Spanish
than he is in English and best when translated into the South
American Indian language Quechua. That is what Strand's
persona wants. He says to his translator, "Friend, say
something amazing for me. It must be something you take
for granted, something meaningless to you, but impossible
for me to think of." And: "Tell me that my ugly tomb, my
transcending gesture, my way into the next world, your world,
my world made by you, you the future of me, my future, my
features translated, tell me that it will improve, that it will
seem better for my not giving into what passes for style, tell

me that its perpetual prose will become less than itself and
hint always at more." The Monument translated will be "the
last straw taken away"; it will mean the completion of the
persona's program of self-effacement. 61  Mark Strand chooses
to address the future, not as a Canadian-born American citizen who lives and writes in the last half of the twentieth century, but as No One--not the contemptible No Man of The
Odyssey, but the existential everyman that is, potentially,
each of us.

　　　　But the game is more complex than that. The startling
realization is that the book has already been translated; this
is evident from the several translator's notes throughout. Yet
translated from what? The persona tells his translator that
"some will think I wrote this and some will think you wrote
this. The fact is neither of us did. There is a ghostly third
who has taken up residence in this pen, this pen we hold."
Every poet has felt the workings of this "ghostly third," the
thing that at times seems actually to do the writing. Clumsy
writers call it "my gift" or "God speaking through me," but
it is something else entirely. It is the push of experience
toward language, deeds trying to become words and stay deeds.
Howard Nemerov defines poetry as the language spoken in
Eden during the few hours between the naming of Creation
and the Fall; I would say that poetry is the stuff that tries
to be and that at its best comes closest to being that language. And it is the language of Eden, the language that
sometimes takes over and that we personify as Muse, God,
ghostly third, the timeless language that "calls from the future," as the persona says, that is the original language of
The Monument. 62  (The title of the book, incidentally, was
no doubt suggested by Elizabeth Bishop's "The Monument,"
a sort of reverse "Ozymandias" in which a man-made marker
with no name on it seems to transcend and perhaps outlast
nature. )

　　　　So where do we leave the Strand persona this time?
Lost in the tradition is where, sunk in the sea of poetry in
which every true poet is submerged, according to T. S.
Eliot. To make this point, the fifty-second and final chapter
of The Monument consists of quotations from other writers
only. The telling lines are from Whitman: "O to disengage
myself from those corpses of me, which I turn and look at
where I cast them, / To pass on, (O living! always living!)
and leave the corpses behind." 63  The corpses are the poets
of the past and present who do not really exist, whose poetry
does not really exist except insofar as it is the language of
Eden.

With the publication of The Monument, it would seem that Strand has taken his poetic program as far as he can. But perhaps it should be called "a" program instead of "his," which implies a single, career-long plan. As we know, monism and dualism do not exist in pure forms, and a single mind manifests both tendencies. Strand issued another collection of lyrics, The Late Hour, almost simultaneously with The Monument. The appearance of The Late Hour, with its varied concerns, means that Strand has not invested everything in a program of self-effacement that began with Sleeping with One Eye Open and ended with The Monument. The Late Hour contains some of Strand's simplest and most extraordinarily beautiful poems, with titles like "My Son," "No Particular Day," and, unlikely though it may seem, "Pot Roast." It ends with the jubilant "Night Pieces," a poem whose persona sits drinking his morning coffee and awaiting the arrival of The New York Times, with self-effacement the farthest thing from his mind.

Still, both books sprang from the same consciousness, and a certain coherency obtains. Many of the poems in The Late Hour complement the central concern of The Monument. There is "An Old Man Awake in His Own Death," for instance, who describes the afterlife in terms that are "vaguely surreal, vaguely narrative," to borrow from a Strand interview the terms that he uses to describe best his own style. [64] One can hear that same old man's voice in The Monument as well: "A box placed underground with me inside would never be right," he says. "And then I thought of The Monument."[65] It is a consoling voice, at bottom. It is the nonraving of No One who is not dying at all.

## CONCLUSION

---

"I saw that I was just another Robinson Crusoe."

On January 8, 1800, an eleven- or twelve-year-old boy wandered into a small town in southern France. Speechless and naked except for the tatters of a shirt, he behaved like an animal, bolting whatever food he could get, relieving himself wherever he pleased. Taken into custody, he ended up in Paris, where he was taught to behave to some extent but never to speak. After a while, it was decided that the Wild Boy, as he was called, could benefit no further from training, and although he continued to be cared for, little is known of his later life. He died in Paris in 1828 and has since been the subject of numerous studies, popular as well as scholarly, including the celebrated film by François Truffaut.

In The Forbidden Experiment: The Story of the Wild Boy of Aveyron, Roger Shattuck attempts to explain why the Wild Boy "haunts our collective memory."[1] He notes that "the oldest stories, from Egyptian myths and Aesop's fables to Walt Disney, are about animals. Every generation has had its Tarzan and has become excited about stories of wolf children" such as the Wild Boy. [2] A moment's reflection reveals the profundity of this assertion as it applies to narratives from the earliest legends to the latest films. First, there are the near-human animals who seem to be on the verge of speaking to us: King Kong, Lassie, Flipper, Benji, Mr. Ed, Francis the Talking Mule. Then there are their opposites, near-human types who are trying to distance themselves from civilization, such as the yeti and the sasquatch. Next on the evolutionary scale are the primitive but reliable sidekicks: Pocahontas, Chingachgook, Queequeg, Nigger Jim, Tonto, Little Beaver, Ken Kesey's Chief Bromden, the Wookiee Chewbacca of Star Wars. And finally there are the completely autonomous types who nonetheless retain contact with the na-

tural world: the satyrs and centaurs, Romulus and Remus,
Sts. Francis and Jerome, Mowgli, Rima of W. H. Hudson's
Green Mansions.

All of these characters, whether animals with human
qualities or vice versa, suggest one thing: escape. Shattuck
says that one can escape in one of two directions.

> Children in daydreams and adults in their myths
> and in their deeds reveal a profound wish to fly.
> Icarus' melted wings, Leonardo's drawings, and
> legions of angels and winged creatures proclaim
> our yearning to rise above our lot and glide far
> away. If we could fly, we would achieve ubiquity
> and omniscience, almost a form of salvation lifting
> us above worldly cares to a higher existence. The
> bird that soars and swoops overhead can go any-
> where. We imagine him happy. "Free as a bird,"
> the saying goes. We dream of wings because they
> would bring magic transcendence. 3

Yet there is another way to escape, one that

> looks less attractive at first glance. But I believe
> that it has even wider appeal. At times we wish
> to withdraw into a hole, into ourselves, like turtles.
> We retreat not just from hardship and pain but from
> the simple responsibility of getting up every day to
> face the world as ourselves. How can we go on
> when other people expect so much from us? We
> begin to shrink from our own fragile identities,
> from family and friends, from the whole culture
> that surrounds us like an attentive audience when-
> ever we venture forth. At such moments, any re-
> turn to an earlier and simpler life attracts us,
> especially the kind of existence we believe animals
> have. "I believe I could turn and live with animals,"
> Walt Whitman wrote, "they are so placid and self-
> contain'd." Claude Lévi-Strauss ends his highly
> sophisticated book about the difficulties of studying
> human cultures with a long, wistful sentence about
> "relaxing our grip" in order to glimpse human na-
> ture as it was before thought and before culture
> "in the glance of understanding ... we can some-
> times exchange with a cat. "4

In the story of a modern feral child, The Wild Boy of

Burundi (who turned out to be merely autistic), the psychologist-author relates how many letters he received begging him to leave his charge be and let him grow up in the African jungle from which he was thought to have come. Then the author observes: "I am saddened by the letters. What a grim commentary on our lives! Is life in the home sweet home so punitive that we prefer life in isolation, scrabbling for food, fleeing predators, neither giving nor receiving love? Are people fascinated by John [the name given the Wild Boy] because it appears that he has managed to escape what they cannot?"[5]

Clearly, the answer is yes. To live like John is to escape the whip blows of our culture, the constant urging to be and have the best suggested by the list of advertising superlatives that Jeremy Seabrook compiled (see Chapter 1). The author of The Wild Boy of Burundi quotes (in a chapter entitled "A Secret Longing") a fellow expeditionary to Africa:

> "What a comment on the human condition if a man can come forward and honestly say: I would trade all that society has achieved, all the knowledge that has passed down to me from my forebears, reaching back to antiquity; I would trade my daily comforts, my leisure activities, my family and friends, my work, my hobbies, literature, art, music, in a word, my way of life; I would trade all that to be free in the jungle. Probably no one would so baldly make that trade, but certainly all of us feel that in the bargain with ... Nature, we have given up something."[6]

We cannot, of course, articulate that something. Perhaps it can be expressed only in the language of Eden referred to in Chapter 6. Hence, our undying interest in animals--if we cannot say what it is that we have lost, perhaps they can tell us. In a diary entry, Edith Wharton confessed: "I am secretly afraid of animals--of all animals except dogs, and even of some dogs. I think it is because of the usness in their eyes, with the underlying not-usness which belies it, and is so tragic a reminder of the lost age when we human beings branched off and left them."[7] A creature who is still primitive yet articulate enough to explain himself: no wonder anthropologists trip all over themselves to isolate and study feral children before they turn into creatures who resemble the rest of us.

Of the innumerable figures who seem to be able to function as humans yet retain some sense of union with the natural world, Robinson Crusoe offers a particularly interesting example. Alexander Selkirk, the real-life Crusoe, had marooned himself on one of the Juan Fernández Islands off the coast of Chile following a dispute with his captain. Discovered four years later by an English privateer, Selkirk was dressed in goatskins and could speak little of his native tongue. Noting that Selkirk was more at home with animals than with human beings, the captain of the privateer wrote that "he ... tamed some Kids, and to divert himself would now and then sing and dance with them and his Cats."[8] Embroidering Selkirk's story, Daniel Defoe combines elements that are fundamentally appealing to the overcivilized. Roger Shattuck identifies four basic themes in this first modern "novel": "basic survival in the wilderness, getting away from the stresses of civilized life, preserving a few aspects of human culture, and solitary meditations on the place of man before God and in nature." No wonder Robinson Crusoe represents "the kind of radical cure many of us think we would like to take."[9]

When Crusoe washes up on the American shore, he becomes Hank Morgan, the inventive protagonist of Twain's A Connecticut Yankee in King Arthur's Court. When Hank finds himself adrift in the Middle Ages, he says: "I saw that I was just another Robinson Crusoe cast away on an unhabited island, with no society but some more or less tame animals, and if I wanted to make life bearable I must do as he did--invent, contrive, create, reorganize things; set brain and hand to work, and keep them busy. Well, that was in my line."[10] A typical go-getting American, Hank rewrites the Crusoe story according to his own specifications. Instead of retreating toward the natural state, he advances and insists that others advance with him. A watery Bartleby, Crusoe has quit the world of work and worry; he sings and dances with animals and even resembles an animal. But Hank surrounds himself with creature comforts. He reinvents (or preinvents) the bicycle, the telephone, the stock exchange; in effect, he reinvents, at the height of its technological bustle, the America that so horrified Sigmund Freud.

And it slips beyond his grasp. The empire that Hank Morgan has created so painstakingly slides into war and chaos. The most disturbing element of A Connecticut Yankee is the tone of its final pages, in which Hank slays dispassionately thousands of the enemy. His world gone mad, Hank goes chillingly mad himself. His goal accomplished, he can do nothing else but destroy it.

The following standard abbreviations are used throughout these notes:

| | |
|---|---|
| comp(s). | compiler(s), compiled by |
| ed(s). | editor(s), edition, edited by |
| no. | number |
| p(p). | page(s) |
| rev. | revised |
| trans. | translated by, translator |
| vol(s). | volume(s) |

## Chapter ★ 1

1. Ernest Jones, The Life and Work of Sigmund Freud, ed. and abridged by Lionel Trilling and Steven Marcus (New York: Basic Books, 1961), p. 270.
2. Jones, p. 269.
3. Jones, p. 268.
4. Jones, p. 19.
5. Jones, p. 245.
6. These remarks, as well as the quotations from Hornberger, Matthiessen, Chase, and Young, are from the introduction and the sixth and eleventh chapters of my America's Hive of Honey, or Foreign Influences on American Fiction Through Henry James: Essays and Bibliographies (Metuchen, N.J., and London: Scarecrow, 1980). See also Leslie Fiedler, A Fiedler Reader (New York: Stein and Day, 1977) and Herbert Mitgang's review of Dumas Malone, The Sage of Monticello (Boston: Little, Brown, 1981), in The New York Times, August 11, 1981, C11.
7. Boorstin uses this phrase in his The Exploring Spirit: America and the World, Then and Now (New York: Random House, 1976), p. 33. For a discussion of this and

the other main ideas of the book, see my review-article "America's Eye Problem," Virginia Quarterly Review, 53 (Spring 1977), 371-376.

8. The Illusion of Technique (Garden City, N.Y.: Doubleday, 1978), p. 186. George Baker, in "Language and Mind in the Study of New Religious Movements," ed. by Jacob Needleman and George Baker, Understanding the New Religions (New York: Seabury, 1978), says: "Western science has required a dualistic frame of reference or epistemology, one in which a sharp division was to be made between the subject and the object of knowledge, between the Self that knows and the Not-Self that is known. In contrast, Eastern man has taken his capacity for personal Enlightenment as the primary evidence of his capacity to be moved by the same Spirit of Truth. For this reason, the great traditions of Asia have tended to be socio-psychologically oriented and pantheistic in their spiritual outlooks. Eastern science has required only a monistic epistemology, for the principles that govern the object of empirical investigation are to be discovered in the consciousness of the researcher" (p. 287).

9. These remarks on autobiographical writings derive largely from a Kenneth Woodward interview of John Dunne entitled "Spiritual Adventure: The Emergence of a New Theology," in Psychology Today, 11 (January 1978), 50, 90. Additional material on Descartes is taken from an essay by Robert Bly in News of the Universe: Poems of Twofold Consciousness (San Francisco: Sierra Club, 1980), p. 3, and Will and Ariel Durant, The Age of Reason Begins (New York: Simon and Schuster, 1961), p. 639.

10. A Distant Mirror: The Calamitous 14th Century (New York: Ballantine, 1978), pp. 92 and 94.

11. Literature Inside Out (Cleveland: The Press of Case Western Reserve University, 1966), p. 75.

12. "The Name of Odysseus," The Hudson Review, 9 (Spring 1956), 52-70; reprinted in The Odyssey: A Norton Critical Edition, ed. and trans. by Albert Cook (New York: Norton, 1974), pp. 406-424.

13. "Rimbaud as Capitalist Adventurer," in Bird in the Bush (Norfolk: New Directions, 1959), p. 42.

14. Dimock, p. 411.

15. "Introduction" to Arthur Schopenhauer, Essays and Aphorisms (New York: Penguin, 1970), p. 12.

16. Hollingdale, pp. 14-15.

17. Hollingdale, p. 17. The continued influence of this Platonic-Christian dualism is suggested in Beth Dumas, "Influences of Catholicism upon Social Thought: A Brief

Overview," New Generation 80: A Humanities Review, 2 (Fall 1980), 13-20. Dumas notes that "until the four-teenth century, philosophy was dominated by the church and written from the church's point of view. Renaissance individualism can be seen as a reaction against the discipline of the church and the narrow logic of scholasticism. In a similar manner, the Enlightenment of the eighteenth century can be related to reaction against the church.... Yet much of philosophy so important to eighteenth century politics was influenced by the long domination of the church." Much of Locke, for example, derives from or at least is anticipated by such clerical thinkers as Roger Bacon and Aquinas. Thus, while "Renaissance and En-lightenment philosophers tried to separate philosophy from theology (in reaction to scholasticism, which had tried to incorporate both), they did not escape Christian influence."

When one considers the impact of Locke on American social and political thought, then the distance between a highly idealized classical and Christian dualism and that of this most worldly of cultures does not seem so great. See Merle Curti, "The Great Mr. Locke: America's Philosopher, 1783-1861," Huntington Library Bulletin, no. 11 (April 1937), 107-151, for an overview of Locke's impact on Franklin, Hamilton, Jefferson, and the other Founding Fathers.

18. C. G. Jung, Memories, Dreams, Reflections, recorded and ed. by Aniela Jaffé and trans. by Richard and Clara Winston, rev. ed. (New York: Vintage, 1965), pp. 247-248.

19. Paul J. Stern, C. G. Jung: The Haunted Prophet (New York: Braziller, 1976), p. 179. Stern notes that when he went among the Indians "Jung was hoping somehow to discover that layers of the psyche buried deep in the unconscious of civilized Westerners were still near the surface of consciousness with so-called primitive, archaic tribes. While this was an anthropological fallacy, it was not uncommon in those days" (p. 165).

20. Jung, pp. 316-317.

21. Kenneth Rexroth, "The Jewel Net of Indra: An Inter-view," Zero: Contemporary Buddhist Life and Thought, 2 (1979), 30. A note on the word "Theravada": in the first or second century A. D. a school of Buddhism arose that styled itself the Mahayana (Sanskrit, "Greater Ve-hicle") as opposed to the Hinayana ("Lesser Vehicle"). Those who clung to the old ways preferred the Pali word Theravada ("The Doctrine or Teaching of the Elders") to the insulting Sanskrit term Hinayana. Today the Theravada

school is dominant in Burma, Thailand, and Ceylon, while the Mahayana school survives, in modified forms, in Mongolia and Korea.

The main doctrinal difference between the two schools is that Theravada Buddhism believes in achieving perfection through complete loss of personality; Mahayana Buddhism stresses compassion for and aid to one's fellow sufferers. Since Rexroth's beatnik seems to have been professing Theravadan principles, it is appropriate for Rexroth to point up the strong need for self-discipline called for by that sect.

For these distinctions I am grateful to William Theodore deBary, ed. The Buddhist Tradition in India, China, and Japan (New York: Vintage, 1972), and Thomas Merton, The Asian Journal of Thomas Merton, ed. by Naomi Burton, Brother Patrick Hart, and James Laughlin, with Amiya Chakravarty as consulting ed. (New York: New Directions, 1975).

22. These historical remarks derive largely from Thomas Hoover, Zen Culture (New York: Random House, 1977), pp. 30-31, with some assistance from the glossary to The Asian Journal of Thomas Merton, cited above.

23. Much of what is said here about Zen derives from Shunryu Suzuki, Zen Mind, Beginner's Mind (New York and Tokyo: Weatherhill, 1979). This is not only the best introduction to Zen but also the best book for the adept as well, a point that says less about this book than it does about the nature of Zen itself, in which one is always a "beginner."

24. Hoover, p. iv.

25. Gary Zukav, The Dancing Wu Li Masters: An Overview of the New Physics (New York: Morrow, 1980), pp. 19-20, 41. This book, like Fritjof Capra, The Tao of Physics (London: Fontana/Collins, 1976), and Amaury de Riencourt, The Eye of Shiva: Eastern Mysticism and Science (New York: Morrow, 1981), is one of several that establishes correlations between the new subatomic physics and Eastern religions. As a consequence, it has suffered the attacks of two groups of scientists, a jealous one that does not like to allow interlopers into its domain and a more well-intentioned one that has seen science misused by sloppy thinkers who twist basic scientific principles in order to justify anything and everything. These attacks do not detract from the fundamental usefulness of such books, of course.

26. Zukav, p. 35.

27. Brief, nontechnical summaries of split-brain analysis may

be found in two of the sources cited above: Hoover, pp. 4-5, and Zukav, pp. 39-40.
28. The Stoic and Epicurean Philosophers: The Complete Extant Writings of Epicurus, Epictetus, Lucretius, and Marcus Aurelius, ed. and introduced by Whitney J. Oates (New York: Random House, 1940), p. xiv. Oates's assertion that the perceived world changes does not contradict Hollingdale's suggestion that it stays the same--things can be both static and changeable in that they are continuously replaced by versions of themselves.
29. Oates, p. xx.
30. Oates, pp. xvii-xviii.
31. Oates, p. xxii. Epictetus' idea is honored in the form of a wall plaque that appears in countless American kitchens. Called "The Serenity Prayer," the words are actually Reinhold Niebuhr's elaboration of this fundamental Stoic dictum: "God, give us grace to accept with serenity the things that cannot be changed, courage to change the things which should be changed, and the wisdom to distinguish the one from the other."
32. Quoted in Oates, p. 509.
33. Oates, p. xxiv.
34. Seneca (New York: Twayne, 1973), p. 51.
35. Closing Time (New York: Random House, 1973), p. 30.
36. Elaine Pagels, The Gnostic Gospels (New York: Random House, 1979), p. xv.
37. Pagels, p. xv. All quotations from the gnostic texts themselves are reproduced exactly as they appear in Pagels; thus, all brackets, ellipses, etc. are hers.
   Those with further interest will want to see the full Nag Hammadi texts collected in James M. Robinson, ed., The Nag Hammadi Library in English (New York: Harper and Row, 1977).
   The following scholarly studies are useful complements to the Pagels book: E. R. Dodds, Pagan and Christian in an Age of Anxiety (Cambridge: Cambridge University Press, 1965); Werner Foerster, ed., Gnosis: A Selection of Gnostic Texts, 2 vols. (Oxford: Clarendon Press, 1972, 1974); Robert M. Grant, Gnosticism and Early Christianity, 2nd ed. (New York and London: Columbia University Press, 1966); Robert Haardt, Gnosis: Character and Testimony, trans. by J. F. Hendry (Leiden: Brill, 1971); and Hans Jonas, The Gnostic Religion: The Message of the Alien God and the Beginnings of Christianity, 2nd ed. (Boston: Beacon, 1963).
38. Pagels, pp. 129-130.
39. Pagels, p. 126.

40. Pagels, pp. 130-131.
41. Pagels, p. xxiii.
42. T. G. Bergin and M. H. Fisch, trans., The New Science of Giambattista Vico (Ithaca, N.Y.: Cornell University Press, 1968), p. 414; quoted in Brown, Closing Time, p. 35.
43. The Laughing Savior: The Discovery and Significance of the Nag Hammadi Gnostic Library (New York: Harper and Row, 1976).
44. Dart, p. 117.
45. Quoted in Alfred Kazin, Bright Book of Life: American Novelists and Storytellers from Hemingway to Mailer (Boston and Toronto: Little, Brown, 1973), p. 38.
46. Thomas Merton has translated and introduced many of the sayings of the Verba Seniorum in The Wisdom of the Desert: Sayings from the Desert Fathers of the Fourth Century (New York: New Directions, 1960), and I draw on his introduction for the remarks that follow.
47. Merton, The Wisdom of the Desert, p. 8.
48. Zen and the Birds of Appetite (New York: New Directions, 1968), p. 82.
49. Zen and the Birds of Appetite, p. 83.
50. Moby-Dick (New York: Airmont, 1964), p. 232.
51. The Wisdom of the Desert, pp. 11-12.
52. Peter Mathiessen, The Snow Leopard (New York: Bantam, 1978), p. 19.
53. The Wisdom of the Desert, p. 12.
54. Jones, p. vii.
55. These lines conclude Paul Stern's C. G. Jung: The Haunted Prophet (New York: Braziller, 1976), but how much truer they are of Freud!
56. Life Against Death: The Psychoanalytical Meaning of History (New York: Vintage, 1959), p. 130.
57. Brown, Life Against Death, p. 322.
58. Brown, p. xii.
59. Brown, p. 16.
60. "The Jewel Net of Indra: An Interview--Kenneth Rexroth," Zero: Contemporary Buddhist Life and Thought, 2 (1979), 28.
61. "The Reality of Henry Miller," Bird in the Bush (Freeport, N.Y.: Books for Libraries, 1970), pp. 156-157.
62. Jones, p. 23.
63. Jones, pp. 27, 28, 37, 116; Peter Gay, Freud, Jews and Other Germans: Masters and Victims in Modernist Culture (New York: Oxford University Press, 1978), p. 74.
64. Jones, p. 378.
65. Jones, p. 434.

66. Jones, p. 21.
67. Jones, p. viii.
68. Schopenhauer: Pessimist and Pagan (New York: Brentano's, 1931), p. 10.
69. Arthur Koestler, The Roots of Coincidence (London: Hutchinson, 1972), p. 107.
70. McGill, pp. 26, 100.
71. Essays and Aphorisms, selected and trans. with an introduction by R. J. Hollingdale (New York: Penguin, 1970), pp. 41-42.
72. McGill, pp. 146-147.
73. Hollingdale, "Introduction" to Essays and Aphorisms, p. 34.
74. Quoted in Janet Malcolm, "The Impossible Profession," The New Yorker, November 24, 1980, p. 80.
75. In The Standard Edition of the Complete Psychological Works of Sigmund Freud, trans. from the German under the general editorship of James Strachey, in collaboration with Anna Freud, assisted by Alix Strachey and Alan Tyson (London: The Hogarth Press and the Institute of Psycho-Analysis, 1957), XIV (1914-1916), 306.
76. "On Transience," p. 305.
77. "On Transience," p. 307.
78. "On Transience," p. 307.
79. New York: Pantheon, 1978, p. 72.
80. Jones, pp. 36-37.
81. Malcolm, p. 78.
82. These two quotations from Freud's essay are in Malcolm, pp. 77-78.
83. "On Transience," p. 307.
84. The Great War and Modern Memory (New York and London: Oxford University Press, 1975), p. 8. Other contemporary tragedies are sometimes seen as portentous. R. W. B. Lewis, in describing the sinking of the Titanic in 1912, notes that "the catastrophe was traumatic for the imagination of the Western World. In retrospect one sees it as symbolizing the beginning of the end of 'the beautiful epoch'--of the age of expansion, of psychological and economic confidence, of total faith in science and technology, and of veneration of the very rich.... Henry Adams took the event particularly hard. 'The Titanic blow shatters one's nerves,' he wrote. 'We can't grapple it.' A week later he suffered a stroke largely as a result of it" (Edith Wharton: A Biography [New York: Harper and Row, 1975], p. 322).
85. The mention of Revel as well as the references to Tocqueville and Dana that follow are from my review-article

"Who's in Charge Here?" This essay, which deals with Ronald T. Takaki, Iron Cages: Race and Culture in 19th-Century America (New York: Knopf, 1979), and the larger topic of American versus European ideas of self-control, appears in Virginia Quarterly Review, 56 (Autumn 1980), 742-746.

Chapter ★ 2

1. "Pied Beauty," in The Norton Introduction to Literature: Poetry, ed. by J. Paul Hunter (New York: Norton, 1973), p. 173.
2. The Princess Casamassima (New York: Harper and Row, 1968), p. 224.
3. The Princess Casamassima, p. 268.
4. "A Deal in Wheat," in The Literature of the United States, ed. by Walter Blair et al. (Glenview, Ill.: Scott, Foresman, 1969), II, 516.
5. "A Deal in Wheat," p. 516.
6. The Jungle (Cambridge, Mass.: Bentley, 1974), p. 33.
7. "American Culture," in The American Tradition in Literature, ed. by Scully Bradley et al. (New York: Grosset and Dunlap, 1974), II, 979.
8. Post Office (Santa Barbara: Black Sparrow, 1978), pp. 9 and 115.
9. "Emergency Haying," in The New Naked Poetry, ed. by Stephen Berg and Robert Mezey (Indianapolis: Bobbs-Merrill, 1976), pp. 29-30.
10. "Emergency Haying," pp. 29-30.
11. "The Overcoat," in The Diary of a Madman and Other Stories (New York: New American Library, 1960), p. 71.
12. "The Metamorphosis," in World Masterpieces in Literature, ed. by Maynard Mack et al. (New York: Norton, 1973), II, 1575.
13. "The Metamorphosis," p. 1585.
14. "Bartleby the Scrivener," in Classic American Short Novels, ed. by Martha Heasley Cox (San Francisco: Chandler, 1969), p. 341.
15. "Bartleby," p. 342.
16. "Bartleby," p. 346.
17. "Bartleby," p. 346.
18. "Bartleby," p. 347.
19. "Bartleby," p. 347.
20. "Bartleby," p. 347.
21. Saburo Yamaya, "The Stone Image of Melville's Pierre," Studies in English Literature (Tokyo), 34 (September 1957), 38-39.

22. H. Bruce Franklin, The Wake of the Gods: Melville's Mythology (Stanford, Calif.: Stanford University Press, 1963), p. 135. I have omitted Franklin's footnote numbers; it will be understood that all references to "the Saniassi" are from Indian Antiquities and that the others are from "Bartleby."
23. Franklin, p. 135.
24. Franklin, p. 136.
25. Ed. by M. Thomas Inge (Hamden, Conn.: Archon, 1979), p. 11.
26. Egbert S. Oliver, "A Second Look at 'Bartleby,'" College English, 6 (May 1945), 431-439, argues that Thoreau himself is the model for Bartleby. This identification has angered some prominent members of the Melville establishment, and Oliver is attacked in Alfred Kazin, "Ishmael in His Academic Heaven," The New Yorker, February 12, 1949, pp. 84-89 (73-77 in out-of-city editions); Sidney P. Moss, "'Cock-A-Doodle-Do!' and Some Legends in Melville Scholarship," American Literature, 40 (May 1968), 192-210; and Hershel Parker, "Melville's Satire of Emerson and Thoreau: An Evaluation of the Evidence," American Transcendental Quarterly, no. 7, part 2 (Summer 1970), 61-67. Two studies that emphasize the connection between Bartleby's passive resistance and Thoreau's idea of civil disobedience are Robert E. Morsberger, "'I Prefer Not to': Melville and the Theme of Withdrawal," University College Quarterly, 10 (January 1965), 24-29; and Frederick Busch, "Thoreau and Melville as Cellmates," Modern Fiction Studies, 23 (Summer 1977), 239-242.
27. "Bartleby," p. 353.
28. "Bartleby," p. 349.
29. "Bartleby," p. 354; emphasis mine.
30. "Bartleby," p. 366.
31. "Bartleby," p. 373.
32. Two studies deal narrowly with the element of work in "Bartleby": Louise K. Barnett, "Bartleby as Alienated Worker," Studies in Short Fiction, 11 (Fall 1974), 379-385; and Neil Ross, "Bartleby, Socialist Reformer," Extracts: An Occasional Newsletter, no. 35 (September 1978), 11. The problem with political criticism is that it is almost always reductive. To Barnett, Bartleby is "the alienated worker who, realizing that his work is meaningless and without a future, can only protest his humanity by a negative assertion" (379, emphasis mine). Clearly, there is a Marxist dualism as well as a capitalist one.

Chapter ★ 3

1. Gordon S. Haight, George Eliot: A Biography (New York and Oxford: Oxford University Press, 1968), pp. 66-67.
2. Gordon S. Haight, ed. , The George Eliot Letters (New Haven: Yale University Press, 1954), I, 276-278.
3. This summary of the life of Thomas à Kempis and his best-known work derives from the biographical headnote to The Imitation of Christ, trans. and with an introduction by Leo Sherley-Price (Harmondsworth, England: Penguin, 1977), p. [1]; the entry on Thomas in Sir Paul Harvey, ed. , The Oxford Companion to English Literature (Oxford and New York: Oxford University Press, 1967), 4th ed. , rev. by Dorothy Engle, pp. 815-816; and U. C. Knoepflmacher, George Eliot's Early Novels: The Limits of Realism (Berkeley and Los Angeles: University of California Press, 1968), p. 218n.
4. The Mill on the Floss (New York: New American Library, 1965), p. 301.
5. The Mill on the Floss, p. 301.
6. The Mill on the Floss, p. 301.
7. The Imitation of Christ, p. 31. See also pp. 149-150, the chapter entitled "A Warning against Vain and Worldly Learning. "
8. The Mill on the Floss, pp. 304-305. The ellipses are Eliot's.
9. The Mill on the Floss, p. 306.
10. The Imitation of Christ, p. 29.
11. The Imitation of Christ, p. 33.
12. The Imitation of Christ, p. 68.
13. The Imitation of Christ, p. 109.
14. The Imitation of Christ, p. 104.
15. The Mill on the Floss, p. 306.
16. The Mill on the Floss, p. 308.
17. The Mill on the Floss, p. 309.
18. The Imitation of Christ, p. 116.
19. The Mill on the Floss, p. 308.
20. The Imitation of Christ, p. 136.
21. The Imitation of Christ, p. 41.
22. The Mill on the Floss, p. 455.
23. The Mill on the Floss, p. 470.
24. The Mill on the Floss, p. 482.
25. Quoted in Ellen Moers, Literary Women: The Great Writers (Garden City, N. Y. : Anchor/Doubleday, 1977), p. 265.
26. Moers, p. 265.
27. Moers, p. 267.

28. George Eliot's Early Novels: The Limits of Realism (Berkeley and Los Angeles: University of California Press, 1968), p. 218n.
29. George Eliot's Early Novels, p. 218.


Chapter ★ 4

1. Quoted in Philip Stevick, ed., The Theory of the Novel (New York: The Free Press, 1967), p. 386.
2. Quoted in Philip Rieff, "Fellow Teachers," Salmagundi, no. 20 (Summer-Fall 1972), 11. This essay has since appeared as a book by the same title (New York: Harper and Row, 1973).
3. Rieff, p. 11n. By "Liberation," I take him to mean cults of self-worship rather than legitimate political movements.
4. Rieff, p. 11.
5. Rieff, p. 11.
6. Theodora Bosanquet, Henry James at Work (London: The Hogarth Press, 1924; Garden City, N.Y.: Doubleday, 1928), p. 275.
7. New Haven: Yale University Press, 1976.
8. Proust (New York: Grove, 1957), p. 67.
9. Closing Time (New York: Random House, 1973), p. 105.
10. The Wings of the Dove (New York: New American Library, 1964), p. 342.
11. Quoted by Harold Acton in Nancy Mitford (New York: Harper and Row, 1975), p. xiii.
12. "The Future of the Novel," in The Future of the Novel: Essays on the Art of Fiction, ed. and introduced by Leon Edel (New York: Random House, 1956), p. 33.
13. "Why Think?" The New Republic, February 2, 1974, p. 32.
14. Quoted in Leon Edel, Henry James: The Untried Years, 1843-1870 (London: Hart-Davis, 1953), p. 61. The Esau-Jacob comparison is from p. 245 of the same book.
15. Quoted in Edel, The Untried Years, p. 330.
16. The Portrait of a Lady, ed. by Robert D. Bamberg (New York: Norton, 1975), p. 477.
17. Quoted in Leon Edel, Henry James: The Treacherous Years, 1895-1900 (London: Hart Davis, 1969), p. 331. The emphasis is James's.
18. Henry James: The Master, 1901-1916 (Philadelphia and New York: Lippincott, 1972), pp. 27-28.
19. The two passages that follow are also taken from Hisayoshi Watanabe, "Past Perfect Retrospection in the Style of Henry James," American Literature, 34 (May 1962), 165-181.

20. The emphasis is Watanabe's.
21. The Art of the Novel: Critical Prefaces by Henry James (New York: Scribner's, 1962), p. 51.
22. The Art of the Novel, p. 51.
23. The Portrait of a Lady, p. 27.
24. The Art of the Novel, p. 51.
25. The Future of the Novel, pp. 15-16.
26. Theory of Fiction: Henry James, ed. and introduced by James E. Miller, Jr. (Lincoln: University of Nebraska Press, 1972), p. 152. James was a prolific if unsytematic critic. This book brings together his major critical statements in an orderly way; its value is not to be underestimated.
27. Theory of Fiction: Henry James, p. 195.
28. Theory of Fiction: Henry James, p. 3.
29. The Future of the Novel, pp. 12, 13.
30. Quoted in Henry James: The Middle Years, 1882-1895. (Philadelphia and New York: Lippincott, 1962), p. 116.
31. Henry James: The Master, 1901-1916, p. 74.
32. Henry James and the Visual Arts (Charlottesville: The University Press of Virginia, 1970), p. 1.
33. The American (New York: New American Library, 1963), p. 129.
34. The Education of Henry Adams (New York: Modern Library, 1931), p. 163.
35. The Winters essay is in In Defense of Reason (Denver: University of Denver Press, 1947), pp. 300-343, the Wilson one in The Triple Thinkers, rev. ed. (New York: Oxford University Press, 1948), pp. 88-132.
36. Winters, p. 302.
37. The Rhetoric of Fiction (Chicago: University of Chicago Press, 1962), p. 135.
38. These matters are explored in greater detail in my "Two Modern Versions of the Quest," Southern Humanities Review, 5 (Fall 1971), 387-395.
39. The Letters of Henry James, ed. by Percy Lubbock (New York: Scribner's, 1920), I, 184.
40. The Portrait of a Lady, p. 197.
41. The Portrait of a Lady, pp. 295-296.
42. The Art of the Novel, p. 149.
43. The Art of the Novel, p. 143.
44. The Art of the Novel, p. 294.
45. The Art of the Novel, p. 149.
46. "Attitudes to Henry James," The New Republic, February 15, 1943, p. 224.
47. The Ordeal of Consciousness in Henry James (Cambridge: Cambridge University Press, 1967), p. 324.

48. The Turn of the Screw and Other Short Novels (New York: New American Library, 1962), p. 390.
49. The Portrait of a Lady, p. 270.
50. The Other House (London and Hertford: Shenval, 1924), pp. 48, 196.
51. The Wings of the Dove, p. 51.
52. The Golden Bowl (New York: Dell, 1963), p. 273.
53. The Art of the Novel, pp. 182, 110, 179. The full quotation of The Awkward Age reference is interesting both for its elaborate use of circles as well as James's bemused evocation of art's religious dimension. "I remember that in sketching my project for the conductors of the periodical I have named [Harper's Weekly] I drew on a sheet of paper--and possibly with an effect of the cabalistic, it now comes over me, that even anxious amplification may have but vainly attenuated--the neat figure of a circle consisting of a number of small rounds disposed at equal distance about a central object. The central object was my situation, my subject in itself, to which the thing would owe its title, and the small rounds represented so many distinct lamps, as I liked to call them, the function of each of which would be to light with all due intensity one of its aspects. I had divided it, didn't they see? into aspects--uncanny as the little term might sound (though not for a moment did I suggest we should use it for the public), and by that sign we should conquer."
54. The Art of the Novel, pp. 170, 171.
55. The Art of the Novel, pp. 180, 215, 129.
56. The Art of the Novel, p. 52.
57. "Logic and Symbol in the Multi-Dimensional Conception of the Universe," The Middle Way, 36 (February 1962), 152; quoted in Fritjof Capra, The Tao of Physics (London: Fontana/Collins, 1976), p. 159.
58. The first excerpt is from her poem numbered 1129 in The Complete Poems of Emily Dickinson (Boston and Toronto: Little, Brown, 1960), the second from a July 1862 letter to Thomas Wentworth Higginson; both are quoted in The Literature of the United States, ed. by Walter Blair et al. (Glenview, Ill.: Scott, Foresman, 1969), II, 270 and 278.
59. "Little Gidding," in World Masterpieces in Literature, ed. by Maynard Mack et al. (New York: Norton, 1973), II, 1721.
60. Black Elk Speaks, Being the Life Story of a Holy Man of the Oglala Sioux, As Told Through John G. Neihardt, quoted in Emily Morison Beck, ed., Familiar Quotations,

by John Bartlett, rev. and enlarged (Boston: Little, Brown, 1980), p. 701.

61. Quoted as the epigraph to Robert E. Spiller, The Cycle of American Literature (New York: New American Library, 1956), p. vi.

62. Spiller, p. 128.

63. Spiller, p. 128.

64. Richard A. Hocks, Henry James and Pragmatistic Thought: A Study in the Relationship between the Philosophy of William James and the Literary Art of Henry James (Chapel Hill: University of North Carolina Press, 1974), p. 118.

65. Hawthorne and His Mosses, quoted in Familiar Quotations, p. 569.

66. The Portrait of a Lady, p. 182.

67. The Portrait of a Lady, p. 64.

68. The Great Tradition (New York: New York University Press, 1963), p. 144.

69. The Portrait of a Lady, p. 33.

70. The Portrait of a Lady, p. 18.

71. The Portrait of a Lady, p. 17.

72. The Portrait of a Lady, p. 119.

73. The Portrait of a Lady, p. 75.

74. The Portrait of a Lady, p. 193.

75. The Portrait of a Lady, p. 195.

76. The Portrait of a Lady, p. 217.

77. The Portrait of a Lady, p. 251.

78. The Portrait of a Lady, p. 252.

79. The Portrait of a Lady, p. 288.

80. The Portrait of a Lady, p. 291.

81. The Portrait of a Lady, pp. 307-308.

82. Since criticism often reveals more about the critic than about the party criticized, it is interesting to consider the image used by the angry Osmond as he denounces Warburton for "refusing" Pansy: "He comes and looks at one's daughter as if she were a suite of apartments; he tries the door-handles and looks out of the windows, raps on the walls and almost thinks he'll take the place. Will you be so good as to draw up a lease? Then, on the whole, he decides that the rooms are too small; he doesn't think he could live on a third floor; he must look out for a piano nobile. And he goes away after having got a month's lodging in the poor little apartment for nothing" (pp. 407-408). None of this is true, since Pansy does not love Warburton, and he is unwilling to have her unless she does. What Osmond seems to be describing, therefore, is the way he himself would act in similar circumstances.

83. The Portrait of a Lady, p. 442.
84. The Portrait of a Lady, p. 456. As Isabel is led through the convent, this initial feeling of hers is reinforced: "All these departments were solid and bare, light and clean; so, thought Isabel, are the great penal establishments" (p. 460).
85. The Portrait of a Lady, p. 74.
86. The Portrait of a Lady, p. 115.
87. The Portrait of a Lady, pp. 108, 109.
88. The Portrait of a Lady, p. 386.
89. The Portrait of a Lady, p. 441.
90. The Portrait of a Lady, pp. 337, 338.
91. The Portrait of a Lady, p. 144.
92. The Portrait of a Lady, p. 417.
93. The Portrait of a Lady, p. 489.
94. William Veeder, Henry James--The Lesson of the Master: Popular Fiction and Personal Style in the Nineteenth Century (Chicago: University of Chicago Press, 1975), pp. 120-121.
95. The Portrait of a Lady, pp. 342-343.
96. A useful scientific study of meditation is Herbert Benson, M.D., with Miriam Z. Klipper, The Relaxation Response (New York: Avon, 1975). Benson, Associate Professor of Medicine at the Harvard Medical School and Director of the Hypertension Section of Boston's Beth Israel Hospital, tested a group of meditators for changes in oxygen consumption, brain waves, lactate level, heart rate, and respiration rate and determined that meditation resulted in decreased activity of the sympathetic nervous system and an overall hypometabolic state. Benson then extrapolated a simple meditation technique that has no religious or philosophic overtones and is based on four basic elements: a quiet environment, a passive attitude, a comfortable position, and an object to dwell upon. (In Isabel's case, the object of contemplation is the drawing-room scene involving Osmond and Merle rather than the Pansy-Warburton engagement, which is the object assigned by Osmond.)
97. The Portrait of a Lady, pp. 354, 355, 356, 359, 360, 364.
98. The Portrait of a Lady, pp. 450-453. William Veeder provides a pedigree for Madame Merle that is almost as impressive as Osmond's. For instance, he notes that the names of villainous characters often begin with "M" and then gives thirty-eight examples. He also cites five places in the text where Madame Merle's smile is described as curving to the left and then notes

that "the crooked curl of the villain's sardonic smile derives ... from Milton's Satan and reappears in Byron, Scott, and in virtually every popular novel that I know" (Henry James--The Lesson of the Master, pp. 121-123).

99. These quotations as well as the comments on Daniel J. Schneider's The Crystal Cage (see below) are from an untitled review-article by me that appeared in The Henry James Review, 1 (November 1979), 102-105.

100. I have quoted from James extensively; a representative quotation from Roosevelt might contrast these two American types more precisely than do their opinions of each other. On April 10, 1899, Roosevelt explained American intervention in the Philippines to the members of the Hamilton Club in Chicago; his address is entitled "The Strenuous Life": "The timid man, the lazy man, the man who distrusts his country, the overcivilized man, who has lost the great fighting, masterful virtues, the ignorant man, and the man of dull mind ... --all these, of course, shrink from seeing the nation undertake its new duties; shrink from seeing us build a navy and an army adequate to our needs; shrink from seeing us do our share of the world's work, by bringing order out of chaos in the great, fair tropic islands from which the valor of our soldiers and sailors has driven the Spanish flag." This quotation is from my "Who's in Charge Here?" Virginia Quarterly Review, 56 (Autumn 1980), 742-746.

101. Sallie Sears, The Negative Imagination: Form and Perspective in the Novels of Henry James (Ithaca, N.Y.: Cornell University Press, 1968); Quentin Anderson, The Imperial Self: An Essay in American Literary and Cultural History (New York: Knopf, 1971).

102. Lawrence: Regents Press of Kansas, 1978.

103. Charles R. Anderson, Person, Place, and Thing in Henry James's Novels (Durham, N.C.: Duke University Press, 1977); Robert L. Gale, The Caught Image: Figurative Language in the Fiction of Henry James (Chapel Hill: University of North Carolina Press, 1964); and Philip M. Weinstein, Henry James and the Requirements of the Imagination (Cambridge: Harvard University Press, 1971).

104. The Portrait of a Lady, p. 23.


Chapter ★ 5

1. The Portrait of a Lady, ed. by Robert D. Bamberg (New York: Norton, 1975), p. 296.

2. Heart of Darkness and The Secret Sharer by Joseph Conrad, ed. by Franklin Walker (New York: Bantam, 1969), pp. 3, 132.
3. Heart of Darkness, pp. 5-6.
4. Heart of Darkness, pp. 4, 9, 131.
5. Heart of Darkness, p. 4.
6. Heart of Darkness, p. 9.
7. Heart of Darkness, p. 18.
8. Heart of Darkness, pp. 25, 26, 28, 42, 37.
9. Heart of Darkness, pp. 30, 41.
10. Heart of Darkness, p. 82; my emphasis.
11. Heart of Darkness, p. 93.
12. Heart of Darkness, pp. 84, 97.
13. Fiction and the Colonial Experience (Totowa, N. J. : Rowman and Littlefield, 1973), p. 64.
14. Heart of Darkness, p. 84.
15. The Wisdom of the Desert: Sayings from the Desert Fathers of the Fourth Century (New York: New Directions, 1960), pp. 11-12.
16. In White Night (New York: Rawson, Wade, 1979), John Peer Nugent mentions a State Department official who saw parallels between Hitler and Jones: "the blind dedication, the racism, the thought control, the growing madness in the end--even the use of cyanide by some in the Führer's bunker under the Chancellery Gardens in 1945" (p. 4). In the following pages, the lack of self-worth felt by Jones's disciples will be explored, and that is another similarity between the two cases--Hitler could not have come to power in the manner in which he did were he not able to prey upon the sense of worthlessness felt by the Germans following the Treaty of Versailles. A final similarity is that Hitler, like Jones, insisted on loyalty to himself rather than to the state or to some ideal. The oath required of the Hitler Youth says, "In the presence of this blood banner, which represents our Führer, I swear to devote all my energies and my strength to the saviour of our country, Adolf Hitler. I am ready and willing to give up my life for him, so help me God."
17. White Night, p. 19.
18. James Reston, Jr. , "Jann," Carolina Quarterly, 33 (Winter 1981), 24-25. This is an excerpt from Reston's Our Father Who Art in Hell: The Life and Death of Jim Jones (New York: Times Books, 1981).
19. Reston, pp. 25, 26.
20. Visions of Glory: A History and a Memory of Jehovah's Witnesses (New York: Simon and Schuster, 1978), p. 251.
21. Reston, p. 27.

22. Quoted as the epigraph to Jared Carter, Work, for the Night Is Coming (New York: Macmillan, 1981), p. xiii.
23. John Peer Nugent explains that the devoted saw Jones as "a Black Knight, a Moses in search of a Promised Land for his people. To see himself as a white anything would have been a self-contradiction. Black, he said, was beautiful; White evil. Hence the term White Night for the revolutionary suicide that he claimed would be caused by white bedeviling" (White Night, p. 84).
24. White Night, p. 141.
25. White Night, p. 134.
26. Reston, pp. 44, 41.
27. Heart of Darkness, p. 117.


Chapter ★ 6

1. The Morning Star (New York: New Directions, 1979), pp. 5, 8.
2. Lucien Stryk, "Noburo Fujiwara, Haiku Poet," Georgia Review, 33 (Fall 1979), 590.
3. "Two New Books by Kenneth Rexroth," Poetry, 90 (June 1957), 187.
4. A Meditator's Diary: A Western Woman's Unique Experiences in Thailand Monasteries (Harmondsworth, England: Penguin, 1979), p. 68.
5. Myths to Live By (New York: Viking, 1972), p. 152.
6. The Morning Star, pp. 62, 63, 65.
7. The Morning Star, p. 82.
8. The Phoenix and the Tortoise (Norfolk: New Directions, 1944).
9. In Defense of the Earth (Norfolk: New Directions, 1956), p. 59.
10. With Eye and Ear (New York: Herder and Herder, 1970), pp. 206-207.
11. "Father Rexroth and the Beats," Reporter, 22 (March 3, 1960), 54-56.
12. "The Jewel Net of Indra: An Interview--Kenneth Rexroth," Zero: Contemporary Buddhist Life and Thought, 2 (1979), 26-40.
13. Bird in the Bush (Norfolk: New Directions, 1959), p. 43.
14. The Confessions of St. Augustine, Book VIII, Chapter 7; quoted in Emily Morison Beck, ed. , Familiar Quotations, by John Bartlett, rev. and enlarged (Boston: Little, Brown, 1980), p. 129.
15. I have been unable to locate the source of this quotation.
16. Hesketh Pearson by Himself (New York: Harper and Row, 1965), p. 57.

17. Will and Ariel Durant, A Dual Autobiography (New York: Simon and Schuster, 1977), p. 57.
18. "The Literature of Replenishment," The Atlantic, 245 (January 1980), 69.
19. These remarks are adapted from the preface to "The Oriental Heritage" in my America's Hive of Honey, or Foreign Influences on American Fiction Through Henry James: Essays and Bibliographies (Metuchen, N. J., and London: Scarecrow, 1980), p. 10.
20. J. D. Salinger, rev. ed. (New York: Twayne, 1976), p. 26.
21. Zen in the Art of J. D. Salinger (Berkeley: Creative Arts, 1977), pp. 4-5.
22. "Zen and Salinger," Modern Fiction Studies, 17 (Autumn 1966), 320, 322, 324. In addition to this useful study, see also "Some Zen References in Salinger," Literature East and West, 15 (1971), 83-95, and "Zen and Nine Stories," Renascence, 22 (Summer 1970), 171-182, by the same authors.
23. The notebook passage in which Hawthorne discusses this idea is treated in Oliver Evans, "The Cavern and the Fountain: Paradox and Double Paradox in 'Rappaccini's Daughter,'" College English, 24 (March 1963), 461-463. Evans's point is that in the story Giovanni is not bright enough to see past Beatrice's poisonous interior to her pure center.
24. Franny and Zooey (New York: Bantam, 1964), p. 66.
25. Franny and Zooey, p. 103.
26. Franny and Zooey, pp. 26, 28, 29.
27. Franny and Zooey, p. 30.
28. Franny and Zooey, p. 202. There is a clear contrast between the end of the book and the end of the first half, the "Franny" section, in which Franny is also lying "quite still" but is moving her lips soundlessly, still straining to save herself through the ineffectual Jesus Prayer.
29. Brad Darrach, "Consumed by a Pirhanha Complex," Life, December 11, 1970; quoted in Carolyn Riley and Barbara Harte, eds. , Contemporary Literary Criticism (Detroit: Gale, 1974), II, 313.
30. Sara Sanborn, "Two Major Novelists All by Herself," The Nation, January 5, 1974, pp. 20-21; quoted in Carolyn Riley, ed. , Contemporary Literary Criticism (Detroit: Gale, 1975), III, 363.
31. Walter Clemons, "Joyce Carol Oates: Love and Violence," Newsweek, December 11, 1972, pp. 72-74; quoted in Contemporary Literary Criticism, II, 317.

32. Unholy Loves (New York: Vanguard, 1979), p. 68.
33. Unholy Loves, p. 48.
34. Unholy Loves, p. 254.
35. Unholy Loves, p. 170.
36. Irrational Man: A Study in Existential Philosophy (Garden City, N.Y.: Doubleday/Anchor, 1962), pp. 156-157.
37. Philip P. Hallie, The Paradox of Cruelty (Middletown, Conn.: Wesleyan University Press, 1969), p. 55.
38. Hallie, p. 55.
39. Barrett, p. 285.
40. Barrett, p. 247.
41. The Imitation of Christ, trans. and with an introduction by Leo Sherley-Price (Harmondsworth, England: Penguin, 1977), p. 60.
42. After the Wake: An Essay on the Contemporary Avant-Garde (Oxford: Clarendon Press, 1980), p. 7.
43. Invisible Man (New York: Vintage, 1972), p. iv.
44. Invisible Man, p. 73.
45. Invisible Man, p. 79.
46. Invisible Man, pp. 141, 140.
47. Invisible Man, pp. 71, 105, 77.
48. Invisible Man, p. 154.
49. Invisible Man, p. 433.
50. Invisible Man, p. 455.
51. Invisible Man, p. 456.
52. Invisible Man, p. 547.
53. Invisible Man, pp. 557, 562.
54. Invisible Man, pp. 566, 558.
55. These remarks are from Kinnell's "The Poetics of the Physical World" and are quoted in Stephen Berg and Robert Mezey, eds., The New Naked Poetry: Recent American Poetry in Open Forms (Indianapolis: Bobbs-Merrill, 1976), pp. 133-134.
56. From an anonymous review of Jensen's Bad Boats, in Virginia Quarterly Review, 54 (Spring 1978), 56.
57. Richard Howard, Alone with America: Essays on the Art of Poetry in the United States Since 1950 (New York: Atheneum, 1969), 507-516.
58. Darker (New York: Atheneum, 1976), p. 11.
59. The Story of Our Lives (New York: Atheneum, 1977), p. 8.
60. The Monument (New York: Ecco, 1978), pp. iii, 1, 22, 9.
61. The Monument, pp. 26, 37, 39.
62. The Monument, pp. 38, 46.
63. The Monument, p. 52. The lines are from Whitman's "O Living Always, Always Dying."

64. "A Conversation with Mark Strand," Robert Shaw, ed. , American Poetry Since 1960: Some Critical Perspectives (Cheadle, England: Carcanet, 1973), p. 196. This interview appeared originally in The Ohio Review, 13 (1972), 54-71.
65. The Monument, p. 12.

Chapter ★ 7

1. The Forbidden Experiment (New York: Farrar Straus Giroux, 1980), p. 179.
2. Shattuck, p. 53.
3. Shattuck, p. 180.
4. Shattuck, pp. 180-181. The Lévi-Strauss reference is to Tristes Tropiques, trans. by John and Doreen Weightman, (New York: Atheneum, 1974), pp. 414-415.
5. Harlan Lane and Richard Pillard, The Wild Boy of Burundi (New York: Random House, 1978), p. 43. Lane is the chief author and is thus credited in my text.
6. Lane and Pillard, pp. 178-179.
7. Quoted in R. W. B. Lewis, Edith Wharton: A Biography (New York: Harper and Row, 1975), p. 160.
8. Quoted in Shattuck, p. 193.
9. Shattuck, p. 193.
10. A Connecticut Yankee (New York: Washington Square Press, 1971), p. 44.

# INDEX